WHY RATTLESNAKES RATTLE

WHY RATTLESNAKES RATTLE

RATTLE

... and 250 Other Things You Should Know

Valeri R. Helterbran

Taylor Trade Publishing

Lanham • New York • Boulder • Toronto • Plymouth, UK

Published by Taylor Trade Publishing
An imprint of The Rowman & Littlefield Publishing Group, Inc.
4501 Forbes Boulevard, Suite 200, Lanham, Maryland 20706
http://www.rlpgtrade.com

Estover Road, Plymouth PL6 7PY, United Kingdom

Distributed by National Book Network

British Library Cataloguing in Publication Information Available

Library of Congress Cataloging-in-Publication Data

Helterbran, Valeri R.
  Why rattlesnakes rattle : —and 250 other things you should know / Valeri R. Helterbran.
      p. cm.
  Includes index.
  ISBN 978-1-58979-648-5 (pbk. : alk. paper) — ISBN 978-1-58979-649-2 (electronic)
  1. Curiosities and wonders. 2. Handbooks, vade-mecums, etc. I. Title.
  AG243.H376 2012
  031.02—dc23
                          2011025308

Printed in the United States of America

To Buddy, Rob, Ben,
and my dad,
Richard S. Russell

Contents

PREFACE

*L*ifelong learning is a passion of mine. The longest lifetime is not enough to learn all there is to learn, but that doesn't stop the irrepressibly curious from trying! Reading and thinking may (or may not) be different things. As you read the topic-question responses, contemplate the information within and use it as a springboard for further study or thought. Truly, the most difficult aspect of writing this book was to limit the responses to each topic question—so much information exists on even the simplest of topics and each topic is related to other topics. This work is volume 2 of the original book *Why Flamingos Are Pink . . . and 250 Other Things You Should Know.* Apparently there is no limit to what "should be known!" Many topics in this book may be familiar to you in some ways, yet unfamiliar in others. More than trivia, this book identifies some of the facts, tales, and lore associated with day-to-day living and the world around us. More importantly, this knowledge adds texture and interest to one's general knowledge-base.

The idea for this book, and its predecessor, is rooted in the author's newspaper column, "Things Every Kid Should Know," a weekly feature in her community newspaper, *The Ligonier Echo* (Ligonier, PA). Inspiration for this work was based on continuing requests by teachers and parents to publish a book fashioned similarly to this column for use in the classroom and at home. Furthermore, with the majority of questions and topic ideas being generated by adults to meet their own learning needs, this is truly a book for learners of any age.

Read this book eclectically. Thumb through and read topics that interest you as you see fit. Don't be surprised if you learn something new and interesting. Learning is value-neutral; in other words, the learner makes the judgment as to what is valuable to him or her. Which is more important—learning a new language or learning how to repair a carburetor? The learner is the only one who can ultimately answer this question. Learning adds richness and meaning to our lives regardless of the topic; it should be fun and guided by the learner's interests and needs.

How does one become a lifelong learner or become more of one, you may ask? There are many paths to boosting brain-power. Intellectual fitness is as important in many ways as physical fitness. Some suggestions are noted below:

- ⋈ Read quality books on a regular basis. Vary the types of books and the authors you read. Dabble in books that are fiction, non-fiction, how-to, self-help, philosophical, spiritual . . . the list goes on and on.
- ⋈ Realize that the saying attributed to President Rutherford B. Hayes, *Every expert was once a beginner*, applies to all of us. Small steps yield big results in time.
- ⋈ Teach others! We learn and reinforce ideas best by sharing and working through problems with others.
- ⋈ Make learning a priority. Keep and honor a "to learn" list. Instead of only asking children, "What did you learn today?" add *yourself* to this question. Report what YOU learned today.
- ⋈ Model yourself after the famed artist Michelangelo. He often stated, "I am still learning." Aren't we all?

I hope you find this book interesting and useful. Be a lifelong learner!

—Val Helterbran

ACKNOWLEDGMENTS

A book is almost always the product of minds beyond that of the author. Many lifelong learners contributed topic ideas for this book; others served as consultants for selected areas of interest; and a few stood on the sidelines, lending support in other important ways. Contributors are noted in the bibliographic portion of this work.

My graduate assistant, Jessica B. Syzmusiak, was indispensable in researching topics for this work. As a teacher and lifelong learner herself, her skills and perseverance in this task were extraordinary and much appreciated.

My husband, Buddy, was also a contributing factor in his painstaking proofreading and suggestion-giving throughout the process.

I am also indebted to Debbie Brehun, who continued to support the publication of my weekly column "Things Every Kid Should Know" when she assumed the helm as editor at the *Ligonier Echo*.

In closing, I would also like to thank the many good people at Rowman & Littlefield and Taylor Trade Publishing. This work would never have been possible without the encouragement, support, and hard work of Jed Lyons, Rick Rinehart, Flannery Scott, Alden Perkins, and John Shanabrook.

1

NATURE AND ENVIRONMENT

Do Ants Contribute to the Opening of Peony Buds?

Ants have no direct role in the opening of peony buds. In other words, peony buds will open just fine without the assistance of ants. Ants somehow triggering the opening of peonies is an old wives' tale undoubtedly started because of the common presence of ants on peony buds. These insects are simply attracted to a sweet, sap-like secretion exuded by the bud. This ant activity is very natural and short in duration.

Gardeners are often tempted to spray insecticides on their peonies to kill the ants. However, ants are generally considered harmless to peonies and, in fact, they eat other insects that may be damaging to the plant. Furthermore, insecticides are likely to kill beneficial insects along with the ants. Because nobody wants ants in the house, after cutting peonies for display, a few firm shakes or swishing the cut peonies in cool water should minimize the problem.

What Is Ball Lightning?

Ball lightning is a natural phenomenon associated with regular lightning strikes—but not always—and is a relatively rare natural phenomenon. It often appears as a luminous, hovering sphere drifting horizontally in the air close to the ground or along objects such as telephone wires. Ball lightning has been known to materialize inside and outside of structures (even airplanes!) and lasts from a few seconds to several minutes. It can be orange, red, yellow, or blue in color. Typically the size of a grapefruit, it may be as small as a pea or as large (or larger) than a beach ball. When ball lightning is spent, it dissipates or explodes, disappearing from sight.

Ball lightning is not considered as dangerous as regular lightning, but it is not to be toyed with as it is a high-energy source and has been known to cause damage when directly contacted. Although theories abound, there is no generally accepted explanation for ball lightning and it remains a true scientific mystery, according to *Scientific American*.

Why Don't Birds' Feet Freeze in the Winter?

Ducks walking on frozen ponds or songbirds resting on power lines are a common sight during the winter months. Their feet can tolerate wintry conditions due to a biological heat-exchange feature called *rete mirabile* (Latin for "wonderful net"). This is a fine network of blood vessels in the legs and feet that lie next to or interwoven with each other.

The warm arterial blood heading to the feet from the heart heats up the cooler venous blood returning to the heart from the feet. This countercurrent body system is very efficient in keeping a bird's feet warm without losing much heat from its body core. The blood reaching the feet is warm enough to keep the bird's feet just above the freezing point. Other bird-leg and bird-foot adaptations include having scales rather than skin, very little muscle or nerve tissue, and no sweat glands—all of which help to keep a bird more comfortable in extreme weather.

Why Don't Birds or Squirrels Get Electrocuted on Electrical Wires?

A bird or squirrel can easily walk on an uninsulated wire without being electrocuted. The animal does get a momentary electrical (electron) charge the same voltage as the wire, but no current flows through its body and, therefore, no damage or pain occurs. The bird or squirrel is a poor conductor of electricity (when compared to copper wiring) so the current ignores or bypasses the animal and an electrical circuit is not completed.

Electricity flows from an area of high concentration to an area of lower concentration. If a bird, squirrel, or human for that matter touches an electrical *ground* (an object or area at or near zero voltage), the circuit is completed and current surges through the bird, squirrel, or human on its way to the ground. When this occurs, severe injury or death is the expected result. In short, a squirrel or bird may scamper across an uninsulated wire in perfect health, but if its foot makes contact with a transformer or another uninsulated wire and grounds as the squirrel leaves the line—kaboom!

Why Are Glaciers Blue?

Blue ice is a term most often used to describe areas of a glacier that are blue in color. Glacial ice is formed by accumulated snow that after hundreds of years becomes highly compressed ice and as such is relatively free of air pockets or bubbles. Compressed ice tends to break sunlight into all the colors of the rainbow, like a prism. It quickly absorbs the colors of visible light at the red end of the spectrum. Without the influence of red, the resulting color transmitted to the human eye is blue, often brilliant and deep in color. However, if ice has lots of air bubbles or fractures (because it is less compressed), visible light is reflected and scattered throughout and the ice appears white in color. Dirt, rocks, and other debris are picked up by glaciers as they slowly travel and can give some areas of the ice a gray or brownish color.

Glaciers are the source of about 75 percent of the world's fresh water. They advance or retreat as dictated by climate and can range from the size of a football field to many miles long. In the United States, glaciers are found in Alaska, Washington, Oregon, California, Montana, Wyoming, Colorado, Idaho, Utah, and Nevada.

What Is the Difference between a Carat and a Karat?

Carat and *karat* are both fine-jewelry terms, are pronounced the same, and originate from an Arabic word for "bean pod." The carob (*Ceratonia siliqua*) is an evergreen tree native to the Mediterranean area. The seeds or beans are edible and are now widely consumed as a chocolate substitute. These beans, typically of consistent size and shape, were once used as a basis of exchange in determining the weight and value of diamonds and other gems.

A carat is a measurement of weight for gemstones: one bean equals one modern carat, two beans equals two modern carats, and so on. One carat is equal to 200 milligrams (0.2 grams). Points are assigned for each fraction of a carat so that a quarter-carat diamond, for example, would be described as a 0.25 or 25-point stone. Interestingly, in the Far East, gems were measured against the weight of grains of rice. One grain equaled a quarter-carat diamond. A "four-grainer" was a full carat. This terminology is still used today in some diamond markets.

A karat, on the other hand, is a unit of measure used to determine how much gold is in an item. It is also based on the weight of a carob bean, but when measuring gold, a bean was equal to a unit of 1/24 pure gold, with each karat designated indicating 1/24 of the whole. Pure gold is 24 karat (24K). An item designated 18 karat (18K) is 75 percent pure gold (18 parts pure gold and 6 parts another metal—often copper or silver); 14 karat (14K) means something is 58.3 percent pure gold (14 parts gold and 10 parts another metal); and 10 karat (10K) is 41.7 percent pure gold (10 parts gold and 14 parts another metal). Jewelry is not made of 24K gold because it would be far too soft to stand up to day-to-day wear. In the United States, anything less than 10K is not considered gold.

Does a Centipede Have One Hundred Legs?

A centipede is a segmented arthropod of the class *Chilopoda*. Its body is long, flattened, and features a pair of legs attached to most segments. The first set of legs is modified into venomous fangs or claws to aid it in killing its prey. World-wide, there are about three thousand identified species of centipedes. Most live outdoors in protected, moist areas such as soil, leaf litter, under rocks, and in dead wood.

In the United States, the common "house centipede" (*Scutigera coleoptrata*) is a familiar species as it often inhabits damp basement areas. Its diet consists of cockroaches, clothes moths, and other household pests. With its multitude of long, feathery legs and darting motions, this nocturnal arthropod often evokes fear; however, a house centipede's bite is uncommon and generally causes only temporary, localized pain and swelling in humans.

Centipede is taken from the Latin prefix *centi-* (hundred) and *pedis* (foot). Literally translated as "hundred feet," it is a misnomer because although a centipede may have one hundred legs, it is far more likely that it will have fewer (or more). As stated, this is directly related to the centipede's specific number of body segments. The typical adult house centipede has fifteen pairs of legs.

Also of interest, *millipede* is translated from the Latin *milli-* (thousand) and *pedis* (foot). The millipede, a slow moving arthropod, has two to four pairs of legs per body segment and does not bite. Even the largest millipede will have far fewer than one thousand legs.

What Are Conflict Diamonds?

Diamonds may be a girl's best friend, but some diamonds are mined through the pain and misery of others. The United Nations defines conflict diamonds as "diamonds that originate from areas controlled by forces or factions opposed to legitimate and internationally recognized governments, and are used to fund military action in opposition to those governments, or in contravention of the decisions of the Security Council." In addition to diamonds mined in rebel-controlled areas, diamonds stolen from legitimate diamond mines at the site or in transit for the same purposes may be considered conflict diamonds. With immense amounts of money involved in the illicit mining and selling of diamonds, it should come as no surprise that murder, bribery, torture, counterfeiting, and the like are common.

The region most affected by the conflict-diamond trade is central and western Africa. Funds from these diamonds, also called *blood diamonds*, are also often used to finance conflict elsewhere in Africa, and are suspected of financing some al Qaeda operations. Conflict diamonds are often the product of the forced labor of adults and children. More than four million deaths can be linked to the conflict-diamond trade, not to mention the millions of people displaced from their homelands.

The creation of the Kimberly Process Certification System, established in 2003, was an important strategy to help keep these illicit diamonds from entering the market place. In addition, a *voluntary* system of warranties was designed to make consumers aware that the diamonds they purchase are conflict-free (this is printed on invoices). Due to these steps, the sale of conflict diamonds has been reduced to less than 1 percent of diamond sales. If you are purchasing a diamond, a reputable diamond dealer will gladly share information about the origin of your stone.

What Are Contrails?

Contrails are the cloud-like white streaks in the sky formed by jet aircraft. *Contrail* is a portmanteau word for "condensation trails." Jets emit exhaust in the form of carbon dioxide (CO_2), water vapor, and other matter. When the water vapor emitted freezes into ice crystals, the result is a contrail. However, most of what can be seen as a contrail is not jet emission; it is water vapor already present along the way of the jet's flight path.

Contrails form only at very high altitudes (above 26,000 feet) where the air is very cold and if there is sufficient moisture in the air. If the humidity is low, contrails may form but disappear quickly. It the humidity is high, they remain for extended periods of time

and are called *persistent contrails*. Because winds are often strong at high altitudes, contrails can be "moved" or spread to an area unrelated to air traffic. These human-made, line-shaped clouds grow and spread if the humidity is sufficient and become wispy (cirrus-like) in time. As the sun sets, contrails can appear in beautiful colors due to reflecting or refracting light.

Contrails tend to warm the earth's surface much like other high, thin clouds, but scientists disagree as to whether or not this has any environmental impact. There are no known health hazards associated with contrail formation.

What Is the Difference between a Cyclone and a Hurricane?

Cyclone, according to the National Oceanic and Atmospheric Administration (NOAA), is a term used for a "non-frontal . . . low-pressure system over tropical or sub-tropical waters with organized convection and definite cyclonic surface wind circulation." Generally speaking, in the northern hemisphere, these storms rotate counterclockwise and are called *hurricanes*. The same type of storm in the southern hemisphere rotates clockwise and is simply called a *cyclone*. As an additional point of interest, a typhoon is a type of cyclone that may form in the northwest Pacific Ocean west of the dateline. In short, all of these storms are cyclones but are called different names based on their geographic occurrence.

What Is a Dewclaw?

Cats, dogs, and some hoofed animals may have dewclaws. If present, dewclaws are non-functioning toes located on the inside of the leg and higher than the regular toes. These structures do not touch the ground and are not weight-bearing. Some animals have dewclaws only on their front legs, some front and back, and some even double dewclaws. Dewclaws serve no known purpose.

Animals with dewclaws are prone to injury. Dewclaws can snag on natural and manmade objects outdoors and on carpet and furniture indoors, which causes pain and bleeding. If your pet has dewclaws, it is important to trim these nails as well to decrease the likelihood of harm. Dewclaws are often removed within a few days of birth when the bones, if present, are soft. As an aside, for some breeds, it is important that dewclaws *not* be removed as they are considered a part of the breed standard—the Great Pyrenees and Briard are two such breeds.

The origin of the word *dewclaw* is uncertain. First in print around 1575, it is possibly linked to the Indo-European word *teu*, which influenced the development of the word *thumb*. It is also suggested that they may have been so named because they touch only the dewy surface of the ground (if at all).

What Is a Fire Rainbow?

A fire rainbow is a phenomenon called a *circumhorizontal arc* by meteorologists. A rare occurrence, a fire rainbow is caused by light passing through cirrus clouds when the sun is high in the sky (greater than 58 degrees above the horizon). In addition, because cirrus clouds are made up of ice crystals, the hexagonal, plate-like crystals must be aligned horizontally (parallel to the ground) and must be appropriately thick. Sunlight refracts (bends) when it enters the vertical sides of the ice crystals and exits the horizontal bottoms. The result is a horizontal, rainbow-like natural phenomenon that can span hundreds of miles and last an hour or more. Some of these displays are more brilliant than others, with most being small and of short duration. Most sightings occur in the middle latitudes in late spring and summer.

What Are Flotsam and Jetsam?

The words *flotsam* and *jetsam* describe two different things, yet today are most often used in tandem as part of a singular phrase or term. Specifically, *flotsam* is a nautical term referring to ship wreckage, cargo, debris, or other trash or debris found floating on the sea. Flotsam is most often generated by an accident or shipwreck while at sea. Jetsam (sometimes spelled *jetsom*), on the other hand, may look quite the same, but it is material intentionally thrown overboard to lighten a ship's load, especially in times of peril.

Another interesting seafaring term is *lagan* (lay-gun). Lagan is cargo, equipment, or goods that are cast into the sea (like jetsam). However, the difference is that lagan, which may float or sink, is attached to a float, buoy, or other type of marker so that the goods can be recovered when the danger passes.

The words *flotsam* and *jetsam* came into use in the 1500s and have retained their original meanings. In addition, both, whether used individually or as a phrase, have also come to mean discarded odds and ends, parts and junk, or bits and pieces.

Where Does Helium Come From?

Helium is a gas perhaps best known for filling party balloons. In more serious applications, it is used for arc welding and pressurizing liquid fuel rockets, as a cooling medium for nuclear reactors, in supersonic wind tunnels, and as part of a gas mix for certain diving operations. Liquid helium is used in cryogenics, magnetic resonance imaging (MRI), and superconductivity applications. Helium, scientifically designated *He*, is a noble gas on the periodic table. Noble gasses are characterized by their nonreactive, nonflammable characteristics.

French astronomer Pierre-Jules-César Janssen is credited with discovering helium. While studying a solar eclipse in 1868, he noticed a previously unobserved yellow line in the sun's spectrum. Sir Norman Lockyer, an English astronomer, during the same timeframe reported parallel findings through his own studies. Lockyer named this new element *Helium* after Helius, the Greek god of the sun.

Helium is the second most abundant element in our universe, second only to hydrogen, yet it is surprisingly rare in the earth's atmosphere. A product of radioactive decay, helium is quickly lost to space due to its lightness. Luckily, helium can be harvested for commercial purposes by isolating it from natural gas supplies. Domestically, helium extraction occurs primarily in Texas, Oklahoma, and Kansas.

What Is Hoarfrost?

Hoarfrost is the feathery or fern-like build-up of ice crystals that forms on branches, poles, wires, grass, leaves, or other objects exposed to the open air. It is the winter version of dew, both of which form when there is more moisture in the air than the air can maintain; the difference is the temperature at which they form.

Hoarfrost forms when the air is brought to its "frost point" by radiation cooling. In other words, supersaturated moisture in the air and the cooling of the air must occur in tandem. Additionally, the objects exposed to the open air must have chilled below the freezing point. The air temperature determines what types of interlocking crystals develop—needles, plates, cups, spines, feather-like, fern-like, or a combination.

Recorded in Old English, *hoarfrost* dates to at least 1290. It is taken from the Proto-Germanic word *har* meaning "grey," "venerable," or "old" as its appearance is reminiscent of an elderly man's shaggy white beard.

Do Lakes Experience Tides?

Tides result from the gravitational pull of the moon and the sun on bodies of water. This event chiefly affects oceans and bodies of water in direct proximity to oceans. Inland lakes, rivers, and the like are simply not large enough to be significantly affected by this pull and therefore do not experience a "true tide."

There is some disagreement within the scientific community regarding using the term *tide* for the Great Lakes and similar bodies of water, but most concede that appreciable water level changes on large lakes result primarily from storm surge, snow melt, and elevated rates of precipitation or evaporation. These water level changes can vary significantly in occurrence and magnitude, unlike the reliable predictability of "true tides." Water levels can also vary due to a natural phenomenon called a *seiche* (say-shh or sigh-shh). This results when the wind pushes down on one part of the lake; this action, causing other areas to rise, produces waves and an increased water level of, typically, one to five centimeters—similar to sloshing water in a bathtub.

Lake Erie, the shallowest of the Great Lakes, and Lake Superior, the largest, are the most prone to what some refer to as *tides*, but the water level differences are so small, one would need the most sophisticated of instruments to measure them.

Why and How Do Lightning Bugs Produce Light?

The lightning bug or firefly is a nocturnal beetle (member of the family *Lampyridae*). Best known for the ability to produce flashing light, these bioluminescent insects do so to attract a mate. Because there are about two thousand species of fireflies, each species has its own flash pattern—some a single flash, some multiple flashes at given intervals, and so on. This system helps assure that lightning bugs of the same species will find each other. When the male of the species produces a flash, the female, if ready to mate, flashes back immediately in response. He flies closer to her, with both engaging in this type of "light flashing conversation" until they meet.

The exact mechanism of the "lightning" is not clear, but it involves a chemical reaction in special organs in the abdominal region of the lightning bug dedicated to this purpose. Luciferase and luciferin are secreted within the insect. When mixed, these enzymes produce the small flashes of light we see on warm summer nights.

Is There a Difference between a Manta Ray and a Stingray?

Simply put, yes. The manta ray (*Manta birostris*) is the largest of the rays. Its diamond-shaped body can measure twenty-five feet in width, fin tip to fin tip, and weigh up to three thousand pounds. Mantas are commonly, but mistakenly, called *devil rays* due to the distinctive feature of two flexible horn-like structures on their heads. The purpose of these structures is to guide small fish, plankton, and other food items to the manta's broad mouth. Mantas are pelagic (inhabiting the upper levels of the open sea). They live in tropical waters around the globe. They are typically harmless to man as they have no stinging spines; however, if they are startled or injured, their sheer size and power should command respect.

Stingrays, for example the Atlantic stingray (*Dasyatis sabina*), are common in tropical or temperate zones and prefer shallow, coastal waters. They too are diamond- or disc-shaped, but are distinguished by their long, trailing, barbed tail. Stingrays are considerably smaller than mantas. They grow only to a maximum of six or seven feet wide and weigh up to eight hundred pounds, depending on the species. Stingrays spend a great deal of time lying on sandy bottoms awaiting prey to come into range. Stingrays are generally harmless and attempt to flee in the face of danger. However, if stepped on, cornered, or otherwise threatened, they will use their venomous barb for self-protection. This formidable weapon has been known to occasionally kill humans, most notably the "Crocodile Hunter," Steve Irwin.

Why Do Mosquito Bites Itch?

The mosquito (*mosquito* is Spanish for "little fly") is found in most areas around the world. Thousands of species exist. A female mosquito has a long, needle-like structure called a *proboscis*. When she inserts this structure in a victim, she also secretes a little saliva that serves as an anticoagulant to keep blood from clotting. Therefore, she can siphon blood quickly and easily. This saliva is left behind when she is finished and may cause a slight allergic reaction resulting in a pink or red bump and an itching sensation—often intense. In most cases, mosquitoes are simply considered a nuisance, but some carry serious diseases such as West Nile virus, malaria, and encephalitis.

Male mosquitoes drink flower nectar or other sugary fluids. Female mosquitoes will also drink nectar, but far prefer to consume blood and will choose it when given a choice. Mosquitoes may attack birds, frogs, turtles, snakes, and warm-blooded mammals. Some mosquito species consider most any animal as prey; others are quite picky and will draw a blood meal from only specific animals.

Mosquitoes are most active at dawn, dusk, and early evening. To avoid mosquito bites, wear protective clothing and use a safe insect repellant. Eliminating standing water sources on your property also decreases mosquito egg-laying opportunities.

What Is a Pecking Order?

A pecking order is a dominance ranking of individuals or groups within a larger entity like a business, school, organization, or nation. It refers to the relative authority, position, power, or importance of the individuals or groups. This term is taken from the barnyard, where domestic poultry use their beaks to peck each other in order to establish a social hierarchy. Through pecking and being pecked, female chickens come to know where they stand. Once this is determined, chickens submit to being pecked by superordinate birds and peck birds subordinate to them without fear of reprisal. Flocks where a pecking order is established are generally harmonious groups.

The term *pecking order* came to be through zoologist Thorleif Schjelderup-Ebbe when he described this phenomenon in 1921; it began to be applied to humans in the 1950s. Other animals, such as apes, seals, wolves, and many more, also establish a dominance hierarchy through various means. Those at the top of the ranking typically receive preferential feeding and mating choices.

Why Do Rattlesnakes Rattle?

The rattle on a rattlesnake is made of rings of thick, dry scales made of keratin (like fingernails and toenails) that the snake shakes by twitching sets of small muscles on either side of its tail. It is believed that a rattlesnake rattles as a warning, to make its presence known, or to "announce" an imminent strike. However, rattlesnakes can strike without rattling and can rattle without striking.

When a rattlesnake is born, it has a structure on the tip of its tail called a *pre-button*. In a few days, with the snake's first shedding, the pre-button is lost and replaced with a *button*; the button is actually the first segment of the rattle. With two segments (two sheddings), the snake can create a rattling noise. Each segment is loosely connected to the next, so when the snake pulsates its tail, the segments jostle, bounce, and knock against each other, which produces the characteristic buzzing, hissing, or rattling sound. Rattling can continue for hours at a time. Every time the rattler sheds its skin (one to four times a year), a new segment is formed, which makes the rattle longer and louder. However, rattlesnakes in the wild typically have only seven to ten segments as the older segments tend to break or wear off. Therefore, it is generally untrue that one can determine the age of a rattler by the number of segments on its tail. If a rattlesnake's rattle base is damaged or severed, the snake cannot make new rattle segments.

What Is Red Tide?

Red tide is a naturally occurring phenomenon caused by certain types of phytoplankton (microscopic plant-like algae). When the phytoplankton reproduce at a dramatically higher rate than normal (called a *bloom*), they cause the water to take on a discolored cast or surface sheen, typically reddish-brown in color. However, at other times the bloom may be greenish-yellow, purplish, or not visible at all.

Most red tides are not dangerous, but certain algae produce a toxin that can cause paralysis and death to fish and some shellfish. Fish die rapidly and in great numbers if the toxin level is severe, and their bodies can litter the beach or shoreline. Humans can be sickened if they eat red tide–tainted seafood and, due to the release of airborne toxins, can experience severe respiratory distress and a

burning sensation of the eyes and nasal passages. People who suffer from emphysema or asthma are particularly at risk during red tide blooms. Municipalities prone to red tide typically post warnings regarding safety measures.

Red tides occur in coastal regions throughout the world, impacting industries dependent on harvesting sea life. In the United States, coastal areas of Florida and the Gulf of Mexico are prone to blooms; however, blooms are not uncommon up the eastern coast to North Carolina. The exact cause of red tides is unknown, but scientists suspect a confluence of factors including high water temperatures, low rainfall, currents, and low wind conditions. It is difficult to predict the occurrence and duration of red tides, but they are most likely to occur between August and February.

Why Is Salt Used to Melt Ice on the Road in Winter?

Salt lowers the freezing point of water. A 10 percent salt solution freezes at 20°F; a 20 percent solution freezes at 2°F. Melting occurs because there is still water in ice or snow that allows the salt to dissolve into those liquid portions. Salt disrupts the equilibrium between melting and freezing in snow and ice—and melting prevails!

However, salt is most effective in temperatures not appreciably below freezing. If the temperature gets too cold, all the liquid in the ice or snow freezes and the salt cannot dissolve into it and do its job properly. Many municipalities use calcium chloride ($CaCl_2$) as it is more effective in preventing re-icing and is less offensive to the concrete and vegetation with which it comes into contact. However, rock salt as a solid or in solution (brine) is still widely used by itself or in combination with other salts to pre-wet or treat roads before a storm begins, during the storm, and afterward as necessary. In addition, anti-skid material is also spread on roads to aid in traction, depending on the road conditions and weather forecast.

What Is Shellac?

Shellac is a versatile product commonly used as a wood finish. It is available in liquid form, and sometimes in dry flakes. Shellac is produced in its natural orange color or may be bleached to a clear "color." A natural product produced primarily in India and Thailand, shellac comes from the resinous secretions of small, scale insects (*Laccifer lacca*). These insects pierce the trunks of certain preferred trees and drain the sap from the bark. They then secrete *lac* resin, which can be scraped off the twigs and branches for processing into shellac.

Interestingly, it is the only wood finish approved by the FDA as a food because it can be used to coat pharmaceutical tablets and jelly beans, as a fruit glaze, and in food coloring. Because commercially available shellac is typically sold mixed with other chemicals serving as preservatives and stabilizers, it would be unwise, if not dangerous, for consumers to treat it as a food product.

Is It Dangerous to Drive with Snow or Ice on One's Vehicle?

The Vehicle Code of Pennsylvania (HB 121 Section 2, Title 75,) states

> § 3720. Snow and ice dislodged or falling from moving vehicle. When show or ice is dislodged or falls from a moving vehicle and strikes another vehicle or pedestrian causing death or serious bodily injury as defined in section 3742, the operator of the vehicle from which the snow or ice is dislodged or falls shall be subject to a fine of not less than $200 nor more than $1,000 for each offense.

Many states have similar codes. Beyond legal responsibility, common sense and driving experience tells us that driving with an unobstructed view on a road with no impediments creates a safer drive for everyone on the road. "Impediments" would certainly include chunks of snow or ice that fall from a vehicle causing a dangerous situation for the driver of the laden car as well as any others in the vicinity.

What Is Spanish Moss?

Spanish moss (*Tillandsia usneoides*) is neither Spanish nor a moss. Often called *tree hair, Florida moss, graybeard*, or other variations, Spanish moss is actually related to the pineapple. It is an *epiphyte*, or air plant. Plants in this category live on a host plant, but are not parasitic as they make or capture their own food and collect water from rainfall. Spanish moss reproduces when its seeds or small fragments of the plant are blown to other trees by the wind or are carried by birds and insects.

Common in southern areas of the United States (as far north as Virginia), Spanish moss thrives in partial shade in hot, humid climates. If it experiences a long period without rain, the plant will become dormant and revive when moisture is more abundant. Spanish moss has no roots and is characterized by fibrous, thin, scaly stems and leaves that can reach a tangled mass twenty feet in length.

Spanish moss is used primarily today for floral and craft projects. In the days before air conditioning was available or widely used, it was also used to fill mattresses and upholstered furniture as it was considered cooler and more resilient than other materials. It has also been used as packing material, home insulation, a plaster additive, and as privacy screening.

How Do Spiders Make Their Webs?

Different kinds of spiders weave different kinds of webs. For simplicity, only a generalized version of the familiar "wheel-shaped" web will be discussed here. A spider is equipped with (usually) three *spinnerets* on its abdomen through which special liquid protein is pressed from the body, hardening into strong, elastic threads of silk.

Attaching the first thread is typically the most difficult part of web construction as sometimes large distances are spanned by the web. Simply put, if the spider cannot reach the desired attachment point by crawling or jumping, it depends on wind and a lot of luck. The wind blows a thin thread of sticky silk that the spider is exuding as quickly as it can. The spider then crawls back and forth on this primary line, laying down an additional thread of silk each time in order to strengthen it so that it is able to support the rest of the web. Then the spider runs another line to form a Y-shape that results in three main radial lines. From this, it lays down additional radials at a distance apart convenient for it to cross as needed. Now that the non-sticky framework is constructed, non-sticky spiral lines are laid to form the rest of the web.

The spider then eats the non-sticky spiral silk threads and replaces them with sticky silk to catch prey. The centermost spirals (or a preferred area at the edge) are removed and it is here the spider awaits its dinner. This process takes about an hour. The spacing between each spiral is proportional to the distance between the tip of the spider's back legs and its spinnerets. The spider rarely gets caught in its own web as it knows where the non-sticky and sticky threads are and has special, claw-like feet to grasp and release the threads of the web. Spiders can, however, become entangled if startled or if some force violently disrupts the web.

What Are Spring Peepers?

Spring peepers (*Pseudacris crucifer*) are small treefrogs. They are harbingers of spring that make themselves known by way of the males' sharp, trilling, bird-like, peeping mating calls. Peepers emerge from hibernation once the night air reaches about fifty degrees and spring rains commence. To make the characteristic peeping sound, the male fills his vocal sac (located in the throat area) with air. He then forces the air out. The action of taking air in and letting it out makes a peeping sound that can often be heard more than a half mile away. Peepers breed in watery places such as ponds, creeks, ditches, and swampy areas from early spring through early summer. The female lays between nine hundred to one thousand eggs per clutch.

Peepers are small (0.75–1.25 inch), may vary in shades of brown, green, or grey in color, and may have an X-shaped marking on their backs (sometimes indistinct). They have moderately webbed feet with enlarged tips on their digits (toes) and eat small insects, arachnids, and worms. They are found from Nova Scotia through New England and into the southern states through Texas. A different subspecies is found in Florida and Georgia.

For those readers who enjoy the sound of peepers and would like to hear them year-round, visit: www.naturesound.com/frogs/pages/peeper.html.

What Is St. Elmo's Fire?

St. Elmo's fire is a weather phenomenon; it is similar to lightning, but has nothing to do with actual fire. This blue or bluish-white, flame-like luminous vision may appear during thunderstorms (or snowstorms or dust storms) and has the appearance of eerie blue flames. It typically occurs on elevated or projecting structures like lightning rods, church steeples, telephone poles, or the masts and riggings of tall ships. It can also occur on the wings of aircraft if conditions are right.

Early sailors named this occurrence *St. Elmo's fire* after St. Elmo (St. Erasmus), Christian martyr and patron saint of sailors. The phenomenon is well documented by the ancients and early explorers like Columbus and Magellan. Because St. Elmo's fire usually occurs toward the end of a storm, sailors believed they were experiencing heavenly protection by being watched over by St. Elmo.

St. Elmo's fire is more scientifically called a *corona*, *corposant*, or *point discharge*. It was in the 1700s that Benjamin Franklin first correctly recognized that St. Elmo's fire was a result of atmospheric electricity. Essentially, when the air is sufficiently charged, a "glow discharge" is produced that is drawn to a conductive structure or object.

What Is a Sundog?

A sundog (also sun dog) is an atmospheric optical phenomenon characterized by one or two bright spots located close to the horizon at the same elevation as the sun on what is called a *parhelic circle*. Scientifically, these luminous spots are called *parhelia* (sing.: *parhelion*) and occur world-wide. Most easily observed when the sun is low, sundogs result from the refraction of the sun's light through tiny hexagonal ice crystals in the air. More common in cold weather, they appear in some locations more regularly than rainbows.

Although the origin of the term *sundog* is unclear, its first known recorded usage was in the 1631 nautical journal of British naval captain Luke Foxe in his journey to find the Northwest Passage. *Parhelion*, Greek for "beside the sun," has been used to name this phenomena since at least the time of Seneca (4 BC–AD 65), famed Roman philosopher and playwright.

What Is a Tasmanian Devil?

Tasmania is an island state that is part of Australia. One of the animal species found there is a nocturnal, carnivorous marsupial known as a "devil." Devils (*Sarcophilus harrisii*) are solitary animals, but when feeding on a carcass, they congregate and tend to make screeching, screaming noises to establish feeding dominance. Devils also emanate a terrible odor if stressed. They exhibit a wide, gaping mouth or yawn (for which Tasmanian devils are so well known) often mistaken as an aggressive stance; in fact, this display is usually produced if the animal is fearful or uncertain. However, devils do have a hostile temperament and fly into nasty rages if threatened or when competing for a mate. These characteristics are likely what earned them the name *devil* back in the late eighteenth century when Europeans began to settle the island.

Considered a pest in the early days, they were hunted almost to extinction. They are now categorized as a vulnerable species and their numbers are growing again. However, plagued with loss of habitat, competition for food, death by automobile, a new form of facial cancer, predators, and other maladies, only 40 percent survive their first year.

Often likened in appearance to a stocky, wobbling baby bear, devils can grow 20–30 inches in length and weigh 9–26 pounds. They usually have black fur punctuated with a white strip or patch on their chest area and light spots on their sides or rear-end area. Devils feed on any kind of carcass or living rodents, birds, snakes, and other small animals. Their powerful jaws allow them to eat prey in its entirety—flesh, bone, and fur alike.

What Is Thunder Snow?

Thunder snow (also, thundersnow) is an uncommon meteorological occurrence associated with large snow storms. These types of storms occur most frequently in areas located near large bodies of water, such as lakes. March is the peak month for thunder snow in the United States. Thunder sleet can also occur.

Thunder is normally a weather phenomenon linked with the warmer months of the year. However, it can and does occur during the winter months in much the same way when unstable conditions in the atmosphere feature warmer, moister air (relatively speaking) near the ground with very cold air above it. If, under these condi-

Valerie K. Slade

tions, snow-cloud formations develop enough up-and-down motion, thunder snow results. The snow acts as a visual and acoustical suppressant, however. The lightning is rarely seen and the thunder, audible for many miles in a summer thunderstorm, can be heard only within a significantly more limited range with thunder snow.

Why Are Male Turkeys Called *Toms*?

Benjamin Franklin, Thomas Jefferson, and John Adams made up the first committee charged with designing a great seal for America. Jefferson and Adams favored the bald eagle as a lofty emblem of a brave, fierce new country. Franklin disagreed as he considered the eagle to be a cowardly scavenger. He believed the wild turkey to be an elegant, agile, and stately bird symbolizing dignity for the new nation. Franklin, therefore, according to some sources, commenced calling male turkeys *toms* after Thomas Jefferson who opposed him.

Several committees later, in 1782, after a host of other avian choices including the rooster, dove, and phoenix (a mythical bird that rose from ashes) had been considered, the eagle won out in a design submitted by Charles Thomson, secretary of the Continental Congress (now United States Congress).

Do Vampire Bats Really Drink Blood?

Vampire bats are nocturnal, warm-blooded, flying mammals that live primarily in agricultural areas of Mexico, Central America, and South America. As their name suggests, they need blood to survive; in fact, they survive exclusively on blood. Birds, reptiles, cows, goats, pigs, and horses often serve as hosts depending on the species-specific preferences of the vampire bat.

To feed, the vampire bat lands on the ground and hops over to its sleeping prey. Using sensors, it locates a good spot on the prey to feed and makes a small cut with its razor-sharp teeth; it laps, not sucks, the blood as it flows from the host's body. Vampire bats ingest about two tablespoons of blood per feeding. These bats are so efficient and light that they can feed for an extended period of time without awakening the sleeping host. The feeding does not harm the host animal, but bats can cause infection and transmit rabies that can negatively impact a farmer's livelihood. Vampire bats have been known to feed on humans, but very infrequently. If a vampire bat is unable to feed for two consecutive nights, it will die.

The vampire bat's wingspan is about eight inches, but its body is about the size of a human's thumb or big toe. They are clean animals that typically roost upside down in colonies in caves, tree hollows, abandoned buildings, and the like. Its fur is short and ranges from brown to reddish-orange. Recent research suggests that a certain protein found in its saliva may be useful in the treatment of strokes and other human maladies.

Why Do Walruses Have Whiskers?

Walruses are among the world's most interesting animals. They are *pinnipeds* (*pinni* meaning "wing" or "fin," and *pedis* meaning "foot"), as are fur seals and sea lions. The two walrus subspecies (Atlantic and Pacific walruses) live in the Arctic regions and have a lifespan of forty or more years. Small, slow-moving, benthic invertebrates (snails, shrimp, crabs, clams, and worms) constitute their primary food supply. Because walruses can eat up to two hundred pounds of food every day, efficiency in locating food is important.

Tusks are perhaps the walrus's most distinguishing feature. Grown by males and females alike, they are used primarily as "picks" to assist locomotion on land or ice. They also serve to protect the head of the walrus and to stabilize the animal like the runners on a sled as the walrus forages for food underwater.

A walrus also has hundreds of large stiff whiskers (called *vibrissae*) on its muzzle. These whiskers serve as feelers. In fact, a walrus can voluntarily control its whiskers and use them like chopsticks or even fingers to locate and maneuver food or other objects as the walrus searches the muddy seafloor.

What Is the Difference between Weather and Climate?

Weather is a term, meteorologically speaking, used to describe the specific temperature, precipitation, wind, or other factors occurring currently or over the next few days or weeks. *Climate*, on the other hand, is a more general term. It is an average expectation of what one can anticipate weather-wise for an area or region over a given period of time. Climate is calculated by the National Weather Service (and other agencies worldwide) over a period of about thirty years. This offers a perspective to detect any general

shifts in temperature or precipitation, for example. Climates can change over time as we see with the concern over global warming.

The following two sentences illustrate the difference between weather and climate: (1) Although a warm period of weather can occur in Minnesota in January or February, it is probably unwise to plan an outdoor wedding for those months as the climate in that area is typically cold with a high likelihood of snow; or (2) Pineapples grow best in tropical or near-tropical climates, so the prediction of two days of cold weather concerned the growers in Hawaii.

2

THE HUMAN BODY

What Is an Adam's Apple?

An Adam's apple is the larynx or voice box. Its medical name is *prominentia laryngea*. The Adam's apple is made up of the larynx itself and a cartilaginous, box-like structure that surrounds and protects it. During puberty, the larynx of boys tends to grow relatively fast and it sticks out from the front of the throat. As it grows, many boys experience vocal fluctuations—a cracking or squeaky voice—until they "grow into" and adjust to the larger larynx. Some boys continue to have a more pronounced Adam's apple even after puberty. Girls have Adam's apples too, but they are generally not as prominent as in males (although some women do have protruding Adam's apples). Find your Adam's apple by humming while touching your throat until you feel the vibration.

The Adam's apple got its name presumably due to the notion that Adam in the Garden of Eden got a piece of apple stuck in his throat while consuming the forbidden fruit, although biblical scholars today disagree as to what was the forbidden fruit.

Regarding Weight Maintenance, What Is a Calorie?

A calorie is a unit of measurement for heat energy. Scientifically, it is the quantity of heat required to raise the temperature of one gram of water by one degree Celsius at a certain atmospheric pressure. Calories are measured or determined by the heat generated when food is combusted. Food energy is calibrated in *kilocalories* by nutritionists, but most of us simply call these *calories*. Fortunately, food labels detail calorie count and other important nutritional information.

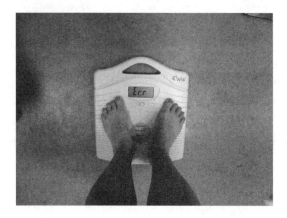

Caloric intake and active fitness routines have received a great deal of attention in the media, schools, and homes across America in the past decade. Most healthcare professionals recommend a sensible diet and daily exercise as essential components of a healthy lifestyle. Essentially, if an individual ingests more calories than the body can use, the extra calories are stored as fat. Fat is essential to good health because it stores energy, cushions organs, helps regulate certain bodily functions, and maintains healthy skin, hair, and nails. However, when too many calories are routinely consumed and the percentage of fat is excessive, individuals may suffer from obesity, which, in turn, may contribute to heart disease, diabetes, and other health problems.

What Is a Charley Horse?

Charley horse (often spelled with a lowercase c) is a lay term for a muscle cramp. Although typically referring to a cramp in the thigh, a charley horse can also occur in other areas of the body. Athletes, or others who "overdo," may experience this phenomenon after performing strenuous or repetitive exercise involving the leg muscles or after physical activity conducted while dehydrated. This painful but short-lived condition usually disappears on its own and may be eased by massage, applying warmth, or stretching the affected muscle or muscles.

Charley horse is an Americanism dating to the 1880s and is likely taken from baseball slang for this frequently occurring condition. The exact origin of the term is unknown, but it is speculated that it came from a lame horse named Charley used to groom a baseball field. Other explanations abound, however. In time, *charley horse* was adopted and used by the general public.

What Is a Conjoined Twin?

Identical twins are the result of a fertilized egg that splits shortly after conception. In conjoined twins, the fertilized egg begins to split, but fails to completely separate. Therefore, two babies are born but they are joined together at the point where the fertilized egg stopped separating. Conjoined twins, more often female than male, occur once in every 200,000 births. About 50 percent are stillborn, and the others have a 5 to 25 percent chance of survival.

Scientists struggled to understand the phenomenon of conjoined twins for millennia. Fear and superstition were common responses to its occurrence because the cause was not understood. Born in 1100, English sisters Mary and Eliza Chulkhurst were one of the earliest documented cases of surviving conjoined twins. Chang and

Eng, born in 1811 in Siam (now Thailand), were perhaps the first set of conjoined twins to become widely publicized. Joined at the lower chest, at which point their livers were connected, they toured as a public exhibition in America and England for Captain Abel Coffin, then later for P. T. Barnum. They became naturalized American citizens during the early 1840s. Both men married (sisters, in fact) and between them, fathered twenty-one children. It is from Chang and Eng that the term *Siamese twins* originated.

Siamese twins is no longer considered a suitable descriptor; *conjoined twins* is the preferred term. Despite medical advances, separation surgeries are dangerous and often impossible. In addition, ethical concerns factor in when it is known that one twin cannot survive the surgery due to shared organs or other critical structures.

What Is Meant by *Double-Jointed*?

People who are double-jointed do not have more joints than others, nor do their joints have twice the normal motion. These folks do, however, have joints, ligaments, and tendons that are considerably more flexible, which allows them to bend or rotate certain body parts in ways most would find painful, if not impossible. They also have shallow joint sockets and smoother-ended bones than most people, which allows them to easily and painlessly dislocate certain joints then return them to their normal positions. The term *double-jointed* dates to the early nineteenth century. More-correct terms are *joint hypermobility* and *joint hyperlaxity*. Elbows, wrists, fingers, and knees are most affected by this condition.

Hypermobility may be an asset to some athletes, dancers, or musicians in their youth (or beyond if they continue to stretch and properly care for their joints). However, individuals with hypermobility tend to experience a higher rate of joint pain when going through growth spurts in their youth and from arthritis as they age. They may also be more prone to joint dislocation and injury throughout their lives.

What Is an Earworm?

An earworm is a little song, jingle, or ditty that gets "stuck" in your head. Despite your best efforts to dislodge the earworm, the song often runs over and over and over again for a few minutes or for days. From the German *ohrwurm* (or-verm), this is also called *stuck song syndrome*, *tune cooties*, or a *sticky tune*.

Perhaps the foremost investigator of this phenomenon is James J. Kellaris, PhD, music scholar and business ethicist at the University of Cincinnati (www.business.uc.edu/earworms). He reports that 99 percent of the population studied experience earworms from time to time. Women (as opposed to men), musicians (as opposed to non-musicians), and worriers (as opposed to non-worriers) report earworms more than others. According to Kellaris's cognitive itch theory, certain types of catchy music (which can be almost anything) act like "mental histamine." The only way the "itch" can be "scratched" is to continue mulling the bothersome music in one's mind—which, like skin, stimulates more "itching," then more

"scratching." Others speculate that earworms are a result of "mental downtime," a simple and temporary loss of mental control.

Remember: An earworm is hearing music in one's own mind; the ear is not hearing the song because the tune is being recovered from the brain's auditory cortex. This is not a medical condition and it almost always dissipates on its own.

Why Don't People Regularly Fall Out of Bed?

Falling from bed is common in young children, especially as they transition from a crib to a toddler or "big" bed. Adults sixty-five years of age and older also experience bed falls and do so at a rate of 1.8 million per year—although most of these incidents are not actually falling from bed while sleeping, but rather falling while getting into or out of bed. Most of us have had the experience or sensation of "catching" ourselves, preventing ourselves from falling out of bed as we sleep, but few of us actually fall.

Although the exact explanation is unclear, Daniel Wagner, MD, medical director of the Sleep-Wake Disorder Center of the New York Hospital–Cornell Medical Center and assistant professor of clinical neurology in psychiatry and neurology at Cornell Medical

School, hypothesizes that we do not often fall because we "are not totally unconscious when we are asleep." He further suggests that there are "certain sensory systems in operation that are able to monitor the relationship of the body to the environment" (http://query.nytimes.com/gst/fullpage.html?res=9D0CE7D81331F93BA25755C0A967958260).

What Is Gout?

Gout is a kind of arthritis that occurs when uric acid builds up in the joints. Uric acid is a chemical created when certain foods and drinks are processed in the body. Examples of these foods and drinks include, but are not limited to, organ meat, anchovies, mackerel, dried beans, peas, asparagus, gravy, cauliflower, and certain alcoholic beverages. Normally, uric acid dissolves in the blood, is processed through the kidneys, and leaves the body in urine. If, however, uric acid builds up in the blood (because the body is making too much uric acid or excreting too little), it can form hard crystals in the fluid around the joints and cause extreme pain, swelling, and inflammation in the affected area. However, many people with high blood levels of uric acid never experience gout.

The big toe, knee, and ankle joints are typically the joints most prone to gout. A gout attack usually begins at night and can last from a few days to many weeks. Some people have only a few attacks in their lifetime, while others have chronic episodes that can cause damage as well as loss of motion in the affected joint. Lifestyle factors, family history, medical conditions, and the taking of certain medications may also increase the likelihood of developing gout. Men are more prone to gout than women; children and young adults are rarely affected. More than five million Americans live with gout today.

Many individuals throughout history have been affected by gout—Henry VIII, Thomas Jefferson, Alfred Lord Tennyson, and Benjamin Franklin to name a few. Anyone having a gout attack should visit his or her healthcare professional for treatment.

Why Does Hair Turn Gray?

Hair color is determined by pigment cells that produce a substance called *melanin*. Melanin determines the color of our hair—black, brown, red, blonde, and the many intermediate shades—based on how it is distributed and the type and quantity of melanin present in each individual hair shaft. All of this is, of course, determined by our heredity, those characteristics passed on to each of us by our parents.

As we age, our hair follicles begin to produce less and less melanin, which typically shows first as gray or silver hair, then white. Also dictated by our heredity is the age at which our hair begins to change to gray or white. Some teenagers may have gray hair or gray patches, while others do not experience this change until their forties or fifties. For most people, it takes a full decade to progress from those first gray strands to being fully gray; some, however,

Photo by the author, permission of Marilyn Deller.

have a much more accelerated process, and others turn gray more slowly. If we live long enough, most, if not all, of us will have a fully gray or white head of hair. Those with light-colored hair turn gray at the same rate as those with dark-colored hair, but the gray is more readily noticed in dark hair.

Although parents often declare that their children's antics have caused their hair to turn gray, there is very little evidence to support this belief. However, certain nutritional deficiencies (such as lack of vitamin B or iron), poor nutrition in general, some cancer or autoimmune deficiency treatments, and smoking can hasten the graying process.

What Is Hyperventilation?

Hyperventilation is an episode of rapid or deep breathing, or both. Sometimes called *overbreathing*, the result is a decrease in carbon dioxide (CO_2) in the person's blood gases. Symptoms of overbreathing may include dizziness, shortness of breath, heart pounding, and tingling of the hands or feet.

Hyperventilation may be triggered by stress, anxiety, anger, depression, emotional upset, or panic. A familiar home treatment for hyperventilation, until recently, was breathing slowly into a paper bag. The thinking behind this involved the paper bag capturing exhaled CO_2 and upon the person's rebreathing it, his or her CO_2 blood-gas balances would be restored. Recent studies challenge the value of this method, however, citing the risk of creating an oxygen deficit (or CO_2 excess) if one overuses bag breathing during an episode. Even more important, because hyperventilation can be a symptom of a serious underlying condition such as lung or heart disease, asthma, or infection, the sufferer may delay critically needed medical treatment by believing that bag breathing will solve the problem.

Anyone experiencing a hyperventilation attack should seek professional medical advice. If serious medical conditions are ruled out, self-calming strategies and breathing exercises are often recommended.

In the Buff: How Did This Phrase Originate?

In the buff is a euphemism for *naked*, *nude*, or a host of other terms used to describe being unclothed. The most likely explanation for the origin of *in the buff* involves a military tunic worn by English soldiers until about the seventeenth century. Called a *buffcoat*, it was made of soft, non-dyed leather that was pale yellowish-brown or tan in color. Presumably, this color was suggestive of the color of Caucasian skin tones, and as early as 1590 and 1602 respectively, poet Thomas Dekker and playwright William Shakespeare used *buff* in ways alluding to nakedness. Another plausible explanation involves the term *buck naked*, which may be derived from the term *buckskin* or the sixteenth-century usage *in stag*, a popular description in that day for being unclothed.

What Is Meant by *Having a Lantern Jaw*?

A lantern jaw is defined as a lower jaw that juts or protrudes beyond one's upper jaw. Although often long and wide, a lantern jaw can also take on the appearance of a long, thin jawline. First used around 1700, the term *lantern jaw* was presumably taken from the elongated form or shape of lanterns of the day. Although it is possible to modify a lantern jaw through cosmetic surgery, many people consider this feature an element of distinction and wouldn't dream of altering it. Two famous individuals with a lantern jaw are Senator John Kerry (D-MA) and comedian Jay Leno.

Why Do Muscles Begin to Hurt Several Days after Exercise?

Muscle soreness that occurs a few days after exercise has a name— DOMS. This is the acronym for *delayed onset muscle soreness*. It is a phenomenon first described by Theodore Hough, PhD, in 1902. Most individuals experience DOMS many times in their lifetime, typically at the beginning of an exercise program, after a change in physical activity, or after strenuous or repetitive physical activity. The severity of DOMS is directly related to the duration and intensity of the causal activity.

Although DOMS can be caused by any type of exercise, activities involving *eccentric* movement seem to be a primary source. Walking or running downhill, landing from jumps, throwing a baseball, or lowering a heavy object (as in a bench press) are examples of eccentric motions. Essentially, muscles are designed to contract. When certain motions force muscles to stretch as they try to contract, microscopic tearing or disruption of the muscle fibers may occur and DOMS results. Current research suggests that the delay in feeling sore or achy can be attributed in part to the slow rate of calcium leakage in the damaged tissues. This leakage typically results in tissue inflammation and pain; other body-repair mechanisms also contribute to DOMS.

DOMS usually includes a range of discomfort that includes muscle stiffness, fatigue, weakness, and decreased range of motion. Anybody can experience DOMS—even those with a good fitness level. Regardless of the severity, most symptoms disappear within five to seven days. Trainers recommend pre-exercise stretching or warm-up motions to reduce the occurrence of DOMS.

What Is the Difference between an Optician, an Optometrist, and an Ophthalmologist?

These three careers all involve vision care, but as terms, they are often used incorrectly. An *optician* is a person who makes lenses, frames, and other optical devices. This professional may verify or fill a lens prescription, make modifications or repairs to vision appliances, help a customer select frames or appropriate vision options, and make adjustments to frames for a proper fit. Becoming an optician typically requires two years of training (additional study is required to dispense contact lenses); opticians are not doctors.

An *optometrist* (also called an optometric physician or doctor of optometry) is responsible for conducting eye examinations, making diagnoses, and treating a number of eye problems or abnormalities. Optometrists *do not* perform eye surgery, but can prescribe corrective lenses and recommend eye exercises to remedy certain eye conditions. Becoming an optometrist requires a four-year undergraduate degree plus a four-year optometry degree. Optometrists must be certified by a national board of examiners and licensed by their state.

Nadine R. Murphy, Sears Optical

An *ophthalmologist* is a medical doctor (MD) or a doctor of osteopathy (DO) with additional specialized training in the medical or surgical treatment of the eye and the prevention of eye diseases. He or she may prescribe medications and can perform surgery on the eye. This includes laser surgeons who perform LASIK surgery and other laser eye procedures. Ophthalmologists typically engage in twelve years, sometimes more, of post-secondary education including the earning of an undergraduate degree, medical school, and residency.

What Is a Placebo Effect?

In pharmaceutical clinical trials, researchers want to know the effects of a new medicine, particularly whether or not the patient experiences relief from the malady affecting him or her. In simple terms, some of the people taking part in the trial get the real medicine (the experimental group); the other people (the control group) get a *placebo* (pluh-see-bo), which is a treatment that should have no effect—saline solution, distilled water, and sugar pills are typical placebos. *Placebo* comes from the Latin for "I shall please."

As part of the procedure, participants know in advance that they may or may not be receiving the actual treatment. Regardless of the trial, researchers have identified something known as the *placebo effect*, which can best be described as the control-group participant or patient experiencing a positive effect from the treatment although the treatment he or she is receiving has no medical value. This can be explained partly by brain chemistry. The body releases narcotic-like substances called *endorphins* when a person is in pain. When a placebo is given for pain-related symptoms, the brain releases endorphins in response, presumably due to the patient expecting relief. As a result, the patient reports feeling better.

Scientists do not fully understand mind-body connections, but when the brain believes something positive is occurring, something positive may occur. It is also speculated that patients associate recovery with being treated by a medical professional, and the brain responds by altering some bodily responses. In addition, patients may improve simply because of a strong positive belief that they will feel better. Regardless of the reason, it is not unusual for one-third of the participants in such trials to show or feel improvement on a placebo.

Interestingly, trial participants have also been known to report negative side effects when taking a placebo where, again, there is no medical reason for this to occur; this phenomenon is called a *nocebo* (no-see-bo) *effect*.

What Is the Difference between Plaque and Tartar?

Plaque is a thin, colorless, sticky film or layer of bacteria on the teeth, gums, and tongue. It can begin to form within as little as four hours after brushing your teeth. Plaque is harmful to dental health because the bacteria involved cause damage to the teeth and other structures in the mouth. Bacteria are naturally occurring organisms in the mouth, but they must be removed regularly for good dental health.

If plaque is not removed, it quickly builds and hardens into tartar or calculus (*calculus* in Latin means a "stone used for counting"). Tartar promotes tooth decay and can create a barrier between the teeth and gums, inviting gum disease and eventual tooth loss. In addition, because tartar is somewhat porous, it often absorbs stains from food which can give teeth a yellow, brown, or otherwise dingy appearance. The American Dental Association (ADA) recommends the following for good oral hygiene:

- brush twice a day with an ADA-accepted fluoride toothpaste
- floss daily
- eat a balanced diet and limit snacks
- visit your dentist regularly

Additional information is available at www.ada.org.

What Causes Red Eye in Flash Photos?

Red eye is a common phenomenon in photographs taken by most amateur photographers. It takes place more often if a flash is used in a darkened environment because the more open the pupils of the eye are, the greater the likelihood of photographic red eye occurring. Essentially, the light of the flash reflects off the eye's retina, which is covered with small blood vessels (these are red, of course). The red-eye effect is more pronounced and occurs more frequently when photographing children or those with a light eye color.

Certain animals, like many deer, dogs, and cats, have a special feature in their eye anatomy called the *tapetum lucidum*. This structure increases the amount of light captured by the retina, reflecting light much like a mirror. This enhances their low-light and night vision. The result can be a bluish, yellow, or white "eye shine" when these animals are photographed. Vertebrates without this structure may show the familiar "human" red eye in photos.

To lessen red eye in photos, look for a red-eye reduction feature when you are purchasing a new point-and-shoot camera; increase the lighting in the area where people are being photographed (if possible); increase the space between your flash apparatus and the camera (if you are using this type of set-up); or invest in computer software that allows you to touch up photos to minimize or eliminate red eye in the finished picture.

What Is Rigor Mortis?

Anyone who watches crime programs on televisions has heard the police or crime scene investigators use the words *rigor* or *rigor mortis* in reference to a deceased crime victim. When a person dies, a biochemical chain reaction begins. The skeletal muscles partially contract and the joints become rigid, or stiff, to the point of being locked in place—this is what is called *rigor mortis* (and it is why we sometimes irreverently call the body a "stiff"). Temperature, physical activity immediately prior to death, amount of body fat, age, and illness affect the onset of rigor mortis. Rigor mortis can begin to set in anywhere from ten minutes to several hours after death and progresses from head to foot. Full rigor is typically reached in 12–18 hours and lasts about 72 hours. A body comes out of rigor when the muscles experience *autolysis*, the natural breaking down of muscle tissue.

The state of rigor mortis is extremely important to medical examiners and criminalists as it can provide helpful information regarding how and when someone died. Mortuaries have massaging and stretching methods to cope with this natural and expected process.

Rigor mortis is Latin for "stiffness of death." In contemporary usage, *rigor mortis* is used exactly as described above, but can also refer to a generalized lack of vitality, energy, or flexibility. For example, "No one is surprised that the company went out of business because rigor mortis seemed to pervade every level of operation."

How Did Sideburns Get Their Name?

Sideburns are areas of facial hair in front of the ears on the sides of a man's face. They were named after General Ambrose Burnside (1824–1881), Union Army commander during the Civil War (and later, governor of Rhode Island and U.S. Senator from that same state). He wore his facial hair in a rather uncommon fashion: as a moustache that connected with his sideburns. He was clean-shaven otherwise. This style was originally called *Burnside whiskers* or *Burnsides*. In time, the usage evolved to *sideburns*.

Courtesy of the Library of Congress, LC-DIG-cwpb-05368

Sideburns may take many forms. They can be composed of short or long whiskers, grown long onto the face or not, or the facial area covered may be thin or wide. They may also be grown long enough to connect with a beard but no moustache (a là Abraham Lincoln). Sideburns may also be called *muttonchops* or *sidebar whiskers*.

What Is a Towhead?

Towhead (also tow head or tow-head) is an Americanism often misheard and misspelled as "toe head" as this is how it is pronounced. Dating to the nineteenth century, it is used to describe a person, often a child, with tousled, light-blond hair. *Tow* is the color of flax, jute, or hemp fibers. Specifically, *tow* refers to the shorter, more

Kelli Jo Kerry-Moran

coarse fibers pulled or combed from the more desirable, longer flax fibers in the making of linen for clothing in colonial times. So, someone with hair resembling tow became known as a towhead, or someone who is towheaded.

What Are the Health Benefits of Walking Up and Down Stairs?

Walking is an excellent form of exercise that can be included in almost everyone's daily routine. The American Heart Association (www.americanheart.org) cites many of the health benefits of walking, including reducing the risk of coronary heart disease and certain cancers and managing obesity and diabetes. Some people include walking stairs (or hills of similar incline) in their regimen.

From a caloric point of view, walking up steps burns more calories than walking down. For example, a 200-pound person burns about 25 calories walking up five flights of steps and about 10 calories walking down them. Walking uphill strengthens cardiovascular function and lowers triglycerides. Research also suggests that walking downhill improves glucose tolerance and, because doing so uses a different set of leg muscles, contributes to maintaining balance.

3

LANGUAGE

What Is Meant by *According to Hoyle*?

Edmond Hoyle (1672–1769) was an English writer and purportedly trained as a lawyer. One of his projects was a reference book of rules and play for card games. He was—and continues to be—the ruling authority on card games and certain other games such as backgammon and chess. Of note, a number of contemporary books feature *Hoyle* in the title, but most have little, if any, association with Hoyle or his original works.

Because of Hoyle's expertise, the phrase *according to Hoyle* was generalized into an idiom signifying following an undisputed authority or following and keeping established rules. Hoyle's name, in short, has become synonymous with authoritative rule-keeping.

Examples of contemporary usage of Hoyle's name are (1) Nan always meticulously researched her scholarly projects according to Hoyle; (2) Randall prepared his taxes according to Hoyle and was sure he would never be in trouble with the IRS; and (3) Carolyn is renowned for her business ethics because she conducts herself according to Hoyle.

What Is Meant by *Dining Alfresco*?

Simply put, *dining alfresco* (al-fres-ko) means "to eat outside." The word is taken from the Italian *al fresco*, translated as "in the fresh [air]." The term *alfresco* can also be used to refer to other outdoors activities, for example, an *alfresco* conference, an *alfresco* spa treatment, or an *alfresco* chess tournament.

Examples of usage are (1) With cooler temperatures and fewer insects, dining alfresco in the early fall is a refreshing experience; (2) When we visited Honolulu, we were delighted to see that there was an alfresco movie theater right on the beach; and (3) The bride was torn between planning an indoor wedding or the alfresco event she had always dreamed of.

What Is Meant by the Phrase *Balling the Jack*?

Balling [or *ballin'*] *the jack* dates to 1913 and a ragtime dance song written by Jim Burris and sung by Chris Smith. The lyrics began and ended as follows:

First you put your two knees close up tight
Then you sway them to the left, then you sway them to the right
. . . .
Swing your foot way 'round then bring it back,
Now that's what I call "Ballin' the Jack."

It was a lively tune accompanied by fast-paced dance moves that imitated the words to the song. Railroaders also used the phrase to mean going at top speed—the "jack" being the locomotive. Originally used to mean dancing or having a great time, it later came to indicate driving, dancing, or conducting oneself in a reckless or fast manner. An example of usage is as follows: "When the trooper clocked him, he was really balling the jack."

Over time, other forms of entertainment further propelled the use of the phrase, notably Judy Garland's and Gene Kelly's film *Me and My Gal* and Danny Kay's rendition of Smith's song *Ballin' the Jack*.

Although the phrase has largely fallen out of use in recent decades, it was bolstered somewhat by author Frank Baldwin's book *Balling the Jack* (1998). In it, Baldwin uses the phase to refer to gambling, specifically, betting everything on a single bet.

What Is the Meaning of *Bellwether*?

Often misspelled as *bellweather*, *bellwether* originally referred to the lead sheep in a flock. This sheep, usually a neutered ram (a *wether*), was fitted with a belled collar. Since the fourteenth century, the term has been used to indicate a ringleader of some sort—often of an unruly or disorderly group. Over time, the definition of *bellwether* has evolved to designate the leader or leading indicator of a trend. It is often used in, among others, the fields of

- finance (i.e., of a stock that is used to gauge the market's performance in general);
- politics (i.e., of people in a geographical area who reflect the sentiments of a nation as a whole); and
- retail sales (i.e., of celebrity clothing that sets the fashion pace).

What Is Meant by Being *Beyond the Pale*?

In contemporary use, *beyond the pale* indicates a behavior that is beyond the bounds of acceptable conduct, decency, or the limits of law. It has nothing to do with coloration (pallor in skin tone) or a pail (bucket). *Pale* in this sense relates to the Latin word *palus*, meaning "stake." We see other uses for this root word in *impaled*, *palisade*, and *pole*. Centuries ago, the stakes driven into the ground to build a fence were called *pales*. These pales came to represent the barrier made by the fence and implied protection, defense, and enclosure within. From that, it was presumed that civilization, safety, and a sense of home were enclosed within the pales.

In time, the term *pale* became more figurative and synonymous with that of a territory or jurisdiction, including an area meant to restrict or confine certain peoples. Notably, a region in fourteenth- and fifteenth-century Ireland of about twenty miles around Dublin (called the *Pale*, or the *English Pale*) was fortified to protect against Gaelic forces or influence. Similarly, the territory around Calais, France, in the fifteenth century was once claimed by the British and fortified as a pale against French incursion. Later in eighteenth-century Russia, in order to restrict trade between Jews and native Russians, Catherine the Great created a region known as the "Pale of Settlement" where most Jews were required to live.

What Is a Blackguard?

A blackguard (blah-gurd) is a low, unprincipled, or contemptible person, often one who uses abusive or profane language. It is speculated that the "black" in *blackguard* refers to the person's soul or character. Another theory involves the term *blackguard* being somehow related to the black uniforms worn by the special guards of the king.

In the fifteenth century, blackguards were unskilled, menial workers who traveled with armies to prepare food or who served as kitchen staff. This usage is now obsolete, but the need for a word describing a scoundrel lives on! By the 1700s, *blackguard* had evolved to its current meaning. Regularly used in Ireland and often seen in literature, *blackguard* is less frequently used in American English.

What Is a Bully Pulpit?

President Theodore Roosevelt (1858–1919) is credited with coining the term *bully pulpit* in reference to using the White House as a platform to promote his ideas and agenda. Interestingly, Roosevelt was using the term *bully* in a positive or congratulatory sense, that is, "Bully for you! Great job!" A pulpit, of course, is an elevated podium often used by ministers. In other words, Roosevelt meant that being president offered him a splendid and advantageous stage from which to communicate with the American people and others.

This phrase is often misunderstood and misused today to indicate using the White House to intimidate or aggressively advocate (bully) for the American point of view. The word *bully* is thought to have come from the Dutch word for "brother" or "lover" and has only recently come to mean harassing or threatening behavior.

What Is a Bumbershoot?

Bumbershoot is a whimsical, although mostly archaic, term for an umbrella. It is believed to have first been used in the late 1800s and is simply a combination of re-spelled parts of the words *umbrella* and *parachute*. Although most folks believe it to be of British origin, *bumbershoot* is actually an Americanism. One of the best-known contemporary usages of the word was in the 1968 movie *Chitty Chitty Bang Bang*, when Dick Van Dyke (as Caractacus Potts) sang "Me Ol' Bam-boo" featuring the word *bum-ber-shoo*.

Bumbershoot is used rarely today, but when it is, it is usually to indicate fanciful imagery, such as when a meteorologist says, "Richmonders are advised to keep their bumbershoots handy for the next few days. Downpours are in the forecast." It is also the name of the annual Seattle Music and Arts Festival. The festival website (www.bumbershoot.org) states that "Bumbershoot was chosen as the festival's name as a metaphor for the festival being an umbrella for all of the various arts and performers it encompasses." Others speculate the name is a metaphor for Seattle's notoriously wet weather!

What Is a Cardsharp?

A cardsharp is someone who is skillful at playing or manipulating cards. The term is perhaps most widely used to describe one who is an expert or professional in cheating at cards for financial gain. *Cardsharp* is often spelled *card-sharp* or *card sharp*. Another term, *cardshark*, is used interchangeably with *cardsharp*—and the connection is readily apparent.

Cardsharp is an Americanism first appearing between 1855–1860. However, its roots run much deeper. Interestingly, both *sharking* and *sharping* appeared in the late 1500s and 1600s, respectively, with both meaning to cheat, steal, or swindle.

What Is Meant by *Casting Pearls before Swine?*

Casting pearls before swine has a Biblical origin as is true of so many of our contemporary sayings. Christ said the following at the Sermon on the Mount: "Give not that which is holy unto the dogs, neither cast ye your pearls before swine, lest they trample them under their feet, and turn again and rend you [tear you to pieces]" (Matt. 7:6 King James Version). Although scholars debate exactly what Jesus meant in that context, almost everyone agrees on how it is now used in general conversation. It essentially means that it is pointless to offer items of quality or sacredness to those who cannot appreciate them and for which they will likely resent the giver.

The imagery and meaning of *casting pearls before swine* is perennially popular, and it is applied in comic strips, books, songs, and everyday usage. It is almost always used by those with the "pearls" about those considered the "swine."

Examples of usage are (1) Giving Joanie a three-carat diamond is really casting pearls before swine as she wouldn't know a diamond from a clump of dirt; (2) Don't go out with that creepy Eric, it would be like casting pearls before swine; and (3) For months I tried to teach Sammi to skate, but it was like casting pearls before swine, especially when I learned that she was criticizing my teaching style.

Why Are Cats Said to Have Nine Lives?

The origin of this well-known myth is not clear, but the clues seem to lead to the reverence ancient Egyptians had for cats. According to Egyptian mythology, the god Atum-Ra changed into the form of a cat when he visited the underworld. Atum-Ra was also responsible for generating eight other deities, or nine including himself. The myth is also traced to Basti, a cat-headed Egyptian goddess; however, as a goddess, Basti would have been immortal, and nine lives would not have been enough! An element of luck also plays into the explanation as nine in many cultures is deemed a "trinity of trinities." More likely though, because cats are typically agile, resilient, alert, and have superior balance, their natural abilities add to their seeming *luck*. Cats are renowned for their ability to get out of a scrape with barely a whisker out of place,

Helen Sitler

which no doubt has added to their mystique and reputation for having nine lives.

Étienne-Jules Marey (1830–1904), French physiologist and chronophotographer, conducted experiments to better understand human and animal motion. In one celebrated test conducted in 1894, he held a cat upside down by its legs and dropped it from a certain height all the while filming the action (sixty shots per second). The resulting images showed that the cat immediately began to right itself, maneuvering its head, back, legs, and tail in synchronous fashion. Once upright in midair, it spread its legs to create a parachute-like effect to slow its descent. As a final tactic, the cat bent its legs as it landed, much like gymnasts do, to absorb the shock for a softer landing.

Let it be said: *Cats do not have nine lives.* They have just one life just like all other living creatures and should be treated with great care and respect.

What Is the Origin of *Cat Got Your Tongue*?

The idiomatic phrase *cat got your tongue* is usually asked in the form of a question. It is used when a talkative person for some reason suddenly and noticeably stops speaking, perhaps for reasons such as guilt, embarrassment, being stumped, and the like. First used in the early 1900s, it applied to a child's lack of response to a question about the possibility of him or her being naughty.

The origin of this phrase is grisly (you have been warned), but all three theories cited most often are just that—theories. One probable source of this phrase dates to at least 500 BC in Egypt and other areas in the Middle East when liars, blasphemers, or others committing crimes of vocalization had their tongues cut out and fed to cats who were often kept to rid dwellings of rodents. In the case of Egypt, this represented appeasement of the deities as a form of flesh sacrifice.

Another possible source relates to crime and punishment. It is speculated that the "cat" refers to a popular device of punishment originating in the 1600s. It was common practice to use whipping as a penalty for a number of crimes. However, some devious person designed a whip with nine smaller knotted whips at its end. Designed to lacerate skin and to maximize suffering, the "cat" generally stopped all verbalizations from the criminal, except cries of pain.

A third explanation is related to the second. The military has always depended on secrecy to carry out its missions. The British Navy is no exception, and during the sailing ship era, the mere mention of a flogging with the "cat" would assure a secret's safe keeping.

What Is Meant by *Being Cattycornered?*

To be cattycornered means to be on a diagonal, diagonally across, or diagonally positioned. Sometimes written as *catty-cornered,* *cater-cornered,* *cata-cornered,* *catercornered,* or *kitty-cornered,* among other variations, the word *cater* itself dates to the 1500s. It comes from the Anglicized French *quatre* meaning "four," or "four-

Dave Rotigel

cornered" in its original use. The word *catawampus*, or *cattywampus*, is also used in this sense.

Cattycornered, an Americanism, first came to be used in the South in the late 1800s and indicated that something was askew, out of kilter, or crooked in some way, but came to mean primarily the "diagonally across" definition. The word evolved from *quatre* to *cater* to *catty* in a process linguists call *folk etymology*, where unfamiliar or difficult words assume the form of something easier, more familiar, or more sensible to the speaker.

Examples of usage are (1) Mom wanted the sideboard moved from being flat against the wall to being cattycornered in the northeast angle of the room; (2) The grocery store was built cattycornered in the southwestern quadrant of the shopping mall; and (3) How would the bed look if we placed it cattycornered in the room rather than next to the wall?

What Is the Difference between *Compliment* and *Complement*?

Originally, these two words had definitions similar enough for them to be used interchangeably. Today, however, they have two different meanings, and their usage and spelling is often confused. A compliment is an expression or indication of admiration, fondness, or praise. We pay someone a compliment if we say

- ✷ What a beautiful jacket! or
- ✷ Your voice adds so much to the choir.

On the other hand, a complement is something that completes or accentuates another thing. For example:

- ✷ Béarnaise sauce is the perfect complement to a tender steak; or

❧ My new car is fully complemented with all the latest technology.

An easy way to remember the difference is that *compliment* is spelled with an *i*, so you can think, "*I* love compliments."

What Is a Coup de Grâce?

A coup de grâce (kooh-duh-grahs) is a final straw or decisive finale to a situation. It can also be taken literally to mean a final, and usually merciful, deathblow. Taken from the French language, it means "stroke or blow of mercy." Its original usage signified putting a mortally wounded person out of his or her misery—often a prisoner who survived a firing squad or other form of capital punishment. It has also been used in reference to ending the suffering of a wounded animal. However, contemporary usage typically involves the "final straw" connotation.

Examples of usage include (1) Danny's cut in pay was the coup de grâce in his decision to quit his job; (2) The coup de grâce prompting her purchase of a condo in Florida was the prediction of another harsh winter; and (3) Not making the football team was the coup de grâce in Erik's decision to leave college.

What Is Meant by the Term *Donnybrook*?

Donnybrook is a district located in County Dublin, Ireland. It was once the location of the infamous Donnybrook Fair, established by a royal charter granted by King John in 1204. Beginning on August 26 and running fifteen days, this fair was quite popular and attracted a large crowd year after year. It provided a gathering place for a mix of horse dealers, fortune tellers, peddlers, dancers, and the like. Food and drink of all kinds were in ample supply. Alcohol-fueled fighting, riotous behavior, and general disorder often became widespread after dusk. Its operation was suspended in 1855 due in large measure to complaints from temperance advocates and residents in the area.

Today, Donnybrook is an affluent suburb of Dublin. *Donnybrook*, as it is used now in the language, is often defined as a noisy quarrel or disorderly conduct—particularly a *verbal* fracas or argument rather than a physical altercation.

Examples of usage include (1) When I went to the town-hall meeting of the candidates, I expected a real donnybrook over the main issues; (2) Donna sought a donnybrook when she confronted her roommate about wearing her new evening gown; and (3) I started a donnybrook with my husband when I arrived at the restaurant ten minutes late.

What Is a Doubting Thomas?

A doubting Thomas is someone who requires proof before he or she will believe something is factual. The term's origin is biblical. Thomas, one of Christ's twelve apostles, wanted proof that the resurrection had occurred, not believing that the sightings of others could be true. He declared that he would believe it when he could see and touch the wounds caused by the crucifixion. When Jesus appeared before his disciples a week later, he said to Thomas, "Put your finger here; see my hands. Reach out your hand and put it into my side. Stop doubting and believe"—and so Thomas did (John 20:24–29 New International Version).

We use *doubting Thomas* in far more trivial ways today, but the core meaning remains unchanged. Examples of usage include (1) Pardon the doubting Thomas in me, but let me see your report card to prove that you have a 4.0 GPA; (2) Jackson was such a doubting Thomas, he insisted on traveling to Egypt to see that the pyramids really did exist; and (3) I would like to believe that you did all the laundry while I was gone, but my doubting Thomas side insists on visiting the laundry room to see for myself.

What Is Meant by *Eavesdropping*?

The portion of roof that extends beyond the outside walls is called the *eaves* (almost always used in the plural form). The purpose of this design is to shunt rainwater off the roof and away from the foundation of the structure in order to avoid water damage to the foundation and basement. The Old English for this structure was *yfesdrype* (eavesdrip), later evolving to *eavesdrop*.

Remember, structures of yesteryear were often smaller with a lower-hanging roofline; it would be rather simple for someone to stand next to an exterior wall to listen to conversations within the house while being concealed in part by the eaves from passersby. *Eavesdropping* as a term has been widely in use since at least the early seventeenth century.

Contemporary usage of *eavesdropping* (or *eavesdrop* or *eaves-dropper*) has varied little since its inception. It still means to listen to a private conversation between others, usually secretly and inten-tionally. Eavesdropping can occur inside or outside a building—and more recently, electronically.

How Did the Current English Alphabet Originate?

The word *alphabet* is formed from the first two letters of the Greek alphabet, *alpha* and *beta*. There are about fifty alphabet systems used in the world today. However, most languages use an alphabet derived from the Roman (or Latin) alphabet. In use since about the seventh century BC, this alphabet was derived from the ever-evolving product of an alphabet used by the Etruscans, who borrowed heavily from the ancient Greek language. The Greek alphabet was directly influenced by the Phoenicians who adopted and spread a form of North Semitic alphabet (considered ancestral to most contemporary alphabet systems). Many scholars believe that the core of our current alphabet originally derived from a greatly simplified version of Egyptian hieroglyphics. The Roman alphabet of classical times had twenty-three letters, as was the case with the Etruscan alphabet. The letters *J*, *U*, and *W* were added during the Middle Ages as were lowercase letters.

The Roman alphabet spread in use parallel to the expansion of the Roman Empire. When the Roman Empire collapsed, the Latin language, used primarily by clerics and scholars, fell into general disuse. The alphabet itself, however, continued to be used as different languages emerged.

Latin as a language today is typically confined to certain scholarly works, scientific classifications, religious works and practices, and legal and medical terminology. Many of our current English words and phrases are based on Latin vocabulary.

What Is the Origin of the Expression *It's Not Over until the Fat Lady Sings*?

Credit for popularizing the expression *It's not over until the fat lady sings* is given to Dan Cook (1926–2008), a San Antonio sportscaster. During a televised 1977–1978 NBA playoff series between the San Antonio Spurs and the Washington Bullets, Cook is said to have uttered this statement referring to not jumping to conclusions about the game's outcome (much in the spirit of Yogi Berra's classic saying in 1973 "It ain't over until it's over").

The saying and many variations existed long before Cook's remark and is believed to be an allusion to Wagnerian opera where a corpulent soprano often performed the final aria. As an aside, there is no evidence that added weight helps or hurts the quality of a singer's voice. The trend in opera today is toward more svelte singers to accommodate physical movement and the requisite acting skills.

What Is a Fortnight?

A fortnight is two weeks (fourteen consecutive days). Normally, calendar increments are measured in days from midnight to midnight. However, various cultures have used dawn-to-dawn, noon-to-noon, or sunset-to-sunset intervals to count days. The Teutons (or Teutones), an ancient Germanic tribe, used nights to count days, and it is from them we get the usage of *fortnight* for a two-week period.

The word *fortnight* is a contraction of *fourteniht* (Middle English) from *feowertyne niht* (Old English). A story circulates regarding Roman forts built in northern England along Hadrian's Wall, the notion being that soldiers got to sleep in a fort at fourteen-day intervals while on patrol duty, hence a "fort-night." Little evidence exists to support this version of the term's origin.

Fortnight is still commonly used in England, India, and other parts of the world and is readily seen in literary works, but in America, its use declined around colonial times and it is rarely heard today.

There Is No Such Thing as a Free Lunch: What Is the Origin of This Phrase?

There is no (sometimes *ain't*) *such thing as a free lunch* is a phrase that means there are few things free in this life—most come with expectations or strings attached. In other words, you typically don't get something for nothing; there is almost always a hidden or indirect cost to "free." This phrase dates to the mid-1800s, when taverns would advertise free food to lure in prospective drinkers. Buy a drink and a free lunch will be yours! Not only was the customer required to buy a drink for the "free" food, but the price of the drink was typically higher in order to defray the cost of the food.

Economists entered the debate about this practice and used the acronym, TANSTAAFL (There Ain't No Such Thing As A Free Lunch) or TINSTAAFL (There Is No Such Thing As A Free Lunch).

Milton Friedman (1912–2006), noted American economist, and Robert Heinlein (1907–1988) in his 1966 classic sci-fi novel *The Moon is a Harsh Mistress*, both popularized the phrase, but neither originated it. The phase is widely used in general language today.

An example of everyday usage is "Joseph rejoiced at receiving his stimulus check, but knew that there was no such thing as a free lunch; as a taxpayer, he had paid for the check himself."

What Is a Freudian Slip?

Sigmund Freud (1856–1939) was the famed Austrian neurologist who founded the psychoanalytic school of psychology. Among other things, he was interested in the workings of the unconscious mind. Freud's theories have been challenged and debated over the decades, but his work remains important to this day; he is considered the father of psychoanalysis.

A Freudian slip is the uttering of something that reveals what the speaker is really thinking as opposed to what the speaker intended to say. In other words, this unintended utterance or mistake is thought to reveal the speaker's true thoughts, feelings, or beliefs.

Freud did not name such slip-ups *Freudian slips*. This name was applied by others, likely followers of Freud's work, who saw the parallels between these occurrences and Freud's studies. It was first used in print by American psychiatrist A. A. Brill, who served as Freud's earliest translator.

Examples of Freudian slips include (1) a husband calling his current wife by his first wife's name; (2) a slender person speaking to a heavy person and saying, "As a matter of fat [rather than *fact*]"; and (3) a boy sending an e-mail to his girlfriend saying, "Wish you were her [rather than *here*]." Freudian slip or a simple slip of the tongue? You be the judge.

What Is a Gerund?

A gerund is a noun derived from a verb and it expresses action or state of being. The word *gerund* is taken from the Latin *gerundium* and ultimately from *gerere* meaning "to bear or carry on." As nouns, gerunds may function as subjects, direct objects, indirect objects, and objects of prepositions, for example. Gerunds always end in *ing*. In other words, if a noun looks like a verb and ends with *ing*, it is called a gerund.

Examples of usage include (1) Digging in the garden is my dog's favorite pastime (the gerund *digging* is the subject); (2) He got in trouble for lying to his teacher (the gerund *lying* is the object of a preposition); and (3) Jennifer gives sewing most of her attention on weekends (the gerund *sewing* is an indirect object).

What Is a Glutton?

A glutton is someone who eats or drinks excessively, greedily or more than is required for healthy living. The term dates to around 1225 and the Old French *gluton*, originally from the Latin *gluttire* meaning "to swallow or gulp down."

Gluttony, the act of being a glutton, is considered one of the Seven Deadly Sins. Originated by St. John Cassian (AD 360–435) and refined by Pope St. Gregory the Great (AD 540–604), this listing of sins was created to help better understand human faults and imperfections and to assist a greater self-reflection. The remaining six sins are pride, greed, envy, anger, lust, and sloth. All of these characteristics seem far easier to identify in others than in ourselves!

Over time, *glutton* has also become a descriptive term indicating a person with a great desire, fondness, eagerness, or capacity for something. Examples of usage include (1) Dave hated to attend his family's Thanksgiving feast because after his third helping of turkey and all the trimmings, his cousins started to tease him about his gluttony [*glutton* used in the classic sense]; (2) Sally volunteered for all the tedious projects at work and soon became known as a glutton for punishment; and (3) I am a glutton for excitement and will happily journey to all corners of the earth for adventurous travel!

What Are the Heebie-Jeebies?

The heebie-jeebies are a feeling of anxiety, apprehension, or impending illness. It was coined by William Morgan "Billy" DeBeck (1890–1942), who used the nonsense syllables (called *reduplications*) in his 1923 cartoon *Barney Google*, appearing in the *New York American*: "You dumb ox—why don't you get that stupid look offa your pan—you gimme the heeby jeebys!"

Heeby-jeebys as a descriptor had a widespread appeal, and soon thereafter, it began to appear in other print media and advertisements. In a short period of time, there was a song and dance associated with the heebie-jeebies. DeBeck, born and raised in Chicago, is also credited with other now infrequently heard slang expressions such as *horsefeathers*, *hotsy-totsy*, and *sweet mama*.

Examples of contemporary usage include (1) Danni went out with Josh once, but she said never again; he gave her the heebie-jeebies; (2) Sally said that ever since she got older, night driving gives her the heebie-jeebies; and (3) I don't know what is wrong with me. I have the heebie-jeebies and hope I am not getting the flu.

What Is a Homophone?

Homophones (hoe-muh-fohns) are words that sound alike but are not spelled the same, nor do they have the same meaning. Homophones are a subcategory of homonyms—but the terms are often used interchangeably. From Greek and Latin roots, *homophone* means "same sound." The English language is filled with examples of homophones:

- to, too, two
- tow, toe
- heir, air
- cent, scent, sent

Another subcategory of homonyms are *homographs*, meaning "same writing." In contrast, these are words that are spelled the same but have different meanings and, typically, pronunciations. Examples include

- "How **does** she look that good at her age?" and "The harvesting of **does** has limitations during hunting season."
- "The secretary will **record** the minutes from the meeting" and "I have a **record** album by the Rolling Stones from the 1970s."
- "May I **present** my research findings at the upcoming conference?" and "May I open the **present** from you before my birthday?

What Is the Origin and Meaning of *Juke*?

Juke has several meanings and can be found spelled interchangeably as *juke*, *jook*, and *jouk*. The most widely seen form of *juke* is arguably *jukebox* or *juke joint*. The usage here comes from Gullah, an English-based Creole language, with *juke* or *joog* meaning "wicked" or "disorderly." *Juke* is also used in football and other games to describe a fake or deceptive move—although this usage of *juke* is likely an English variation of *jouk*—to cheat, fool, or deceive (e.g., "He juked right to miss the block.").

Juking is also a slang usage for distorting reality by employing trickery or falsehoods, or for the gaining of power or advantage by those insecure in some way or in a lower position of power (e.g., "The brokerage house juked its books in order to appear more stable."). First recorded in the early 1500s and originating from the Scottish *jouk*, meaning "to bow down," another enduring usage means "to bend, outmaneuver, dodge, or duck" (e.g., "President Bush juked to miss the shoe hurled at him.").

What Is the Origin of the Word *Kidnapping*?

Kidnapping is a word formed centuries ago from two words—*kid*, considered low slang for *child*, and *napping* (likely an alteration of *nabbing*), meaning "to steal or seize." First coined by kidnappers themselves, *kidnapper* was first recorded in print in 1678 and soon was generalized into the verb *to kidnap*. Originally, kidnapping involved the criminal act of abducting individuals—often children—and selling them to unscrupulous sea captains bound for various British colonies in the New World where they would be sold into slavery, forced labor, or indentured servitude.

Although *kid* is now a generally accepted, informal word for a child or youth, *napper* is mostly obsolete. The word *kidnapper* endures, however, and continues to mean to unlawfully seize, detain, or hold a person of any age hostage, usually for a ransom or some other recompense. It is also playfully used for stolen objects such as tree-napping, dog-napping, and the like.

Kidnappings tend to horrify, yet fascinate, the public. A notable kidnapping of yesteryear involved the infant son of Charles Lindberg, celebrated aviator, and, more recently, Elizabeth Smart. The latter case had a happy ending, with Elizabeth being found and returned home safely.

Kit and Caboodle: What Is the Difference?

Kit and caboodle, and a number of variations of this phrase, appeared in the mid-1800s with most references being of American origin. It was widely used during the Civil War and favored by both armies. *Kit and caboodle* remains in use today largely unchanged in meaning.

Caboodle (also spelled *kaboodle*) is an archaic word for "a collection of items or objects" and is likely taken from the Dutch *boedel*, for "inheritance" or "possessions," or possibly from the English *buddle* or *bottel*, meaning "a bundle or bunch of something." *Kit* refers to one's personal belongings or equipment (i.e., tool kit, or mess kit) and is taken from English colloquial speech to mean "a collection." So *kit and caboodle* is a reasonable slang way to indicate the entirety of one's earthly possessions, or a great deal of something.

We also often hear *caboodle* used without *kit* with the same meaning. Either way, the term or phrase is almost always preceded in use by *the whole*. For example, both of the following examples mean exactly the same thing: (1) We threw the whole caboodle in the van in preparation for our vacation; and (2) We threw the whole kit and caboodle in the van in preparation for our vacation.

What Is Meant by *Kith and Kin*?

Kith and kin is a phrase meaning friends and relatives or, in some cases, just relatives. The word *kith* originally meant one's countrymen or native land. Dating to the 1300s, it is now considered obsolete except in association with *kin*. Its contemporary usage is relatively looser than its original meaning. For example: "We invited just about everybody to our wedding—kith and kin, the people we work with, and even a few people we met on vacation!"

What Is the Origin of the Phrase *Knock on Wood*?

Knock on wood is a saying that signifies the wish to bring good luck or to ward off bad luck. Its origin dates to the time of the ancients when oak was sacred to the Greek god Zeus (known to the Romans as Jupiter), the supreme god of the Olympians. Through a number of cultures over time, *knock on wood* most likely evolved from the idea that benevolent spirits resided in or protected trees. Touching trees let the spirits know someone was there, and doing so was believed to bring good luck. This is the origin of rapping our knuckles on something wooden and saying, "Knock on wood." Similar tree-related superstitions existed among the Celts, Chinese, Koreans, Irish, and many others.

Another plausible origin of *knock on wood* relates to the Jews who were persecuted during the fifteenth-century Spanish Inquisition. According to some accounts, the Jews fled to synagogues for protection. Certain knocks upon the wooden doors of the synagogues were devised as secret codes to allow entry. Because this plan saved lives, knocking on wood became a symbol for good luck. The wooden cross of Christianity is sometimes linked to the origin of *knock on wood* as well.

Despite the long-lived practice of knocking on wood for luck, the phrase *knock on wood* itself is somewhat modern. References to *touch wood*, a British usage, can be found in print from the 1800s, whereas *knock on wood*, the Americanized version, can be found from the early 1900s.

What Is Meant by *Little Pitchers Have Big Ears*?

Little pitchers have big ears means being careful about what you say within earshot of young children; they may hear and understand more than you think! As a phrase, it has been generalized to apply to other audiences (your boss, coworker, roommate, etc.). In existence since at least 1546, it appeared in John Heywood's proverb collection: "Auoyd our children, small pitchers haue wide eares." It is believed that *little pitchers have big ears* originated due to the likeness of the human ear to the large curved handles (ears) often attached to small vessels.

Examples of usage include (1) Watch your language around Junior. Little pitchers have big ears; (2) Shhhh! I think my roommate is home, and little pitchers have big ears; and (3) My boss is in the next room. Let's go down the hallway to talk because little pitchers have big ears.

What Is Meant by the Word *Lollygag*?

Lollygag (sometimes *lallygag*) is an Americanism dating to the mid-nineteenth century. It means to loiter, dawdle, putter around, or generally waste time. Its original meaning signified something that was worthless or nonsensical. *Lollygag* was used in this original sense in a poem referring to a dead cow and appearing in Wisconsin's *Sparta Democrat* in 1859:

> *22 Kwarts of milck she give,*
> *As true as Eye dew liv,*
> *but now er 12 Kwart bag*
> *Aint wuth a lallygag,*
> *Poor old thyng!*

Although the origin of *lollygag* is unknown, it is speculated that it may have come from *loll*, originally meaning "to hang loosely" or "to dangle." In addition, *lolly* is British slang for "tongue." Presumably, *lollygag* may have originated due to the exercising of one's tongue at the expense of getting one's work done. Even the contemporary use of *loll* indicates relaxation, for example, "I lolled about on my vacation in Florida."

What Is Mad Money?

Mad money is a small amount of money held or saved for an emergency or a frivolous purchase. The term's first usage in print appeared in 1922 in an article written by Howard Savage on the topic of Bryn Mawr slang. *Mad money* in the article meant money carried by a woman on a date. If things went awry, she had the funds to transport herself home early—hence "mad" money.

In time, *mad money* was generalized to apply to money for any type of emergency need, then finally to money spent on a desired, yet unnecessary item—an impulse purchase.

Examples of usage include (1) Although she owned fifteen handbags, she used her mad money to buy another that she just couldn't resist; and (2) Gary's wife finally convinced him to put his mad money into an IRA, not the new TV he coveted.

What Is the Origin of the Idiom *Marked Man*?

In colonial America, punishment for crimes committed was often a public affair. Stocks, the pillory, whippings, and ducking stools attracted crowds, with those being punished frequently pelted with rotten produce, mud, and other projectiles. Hangings were less common, but were also held as public spectacles with children often being let out of school to witness the event. The purpose of these publicly held shamings or executions was to deter others from committing crimes and to help restore an individual's relationship with God. Wealthy citizens were often afforded the opportunity to pay a fine rather than suffer the aforementioned punishments.

One punishment designed to increase humiliation and forewarn others of certain criminals was to have those convicted of various offences branded with "shame letters." For example, the letter *T* might be burned onto one hand or the forehead of those convicted of thievery as a permanent and public reminder of the offense. If banished from the community, the criminal was likely to face death if he or she returned. Although the term *marked man* was first recorded in 1833, it is believed its meaning derived from these colonial practices resulting in permanent bodily scarring, marks, or disfigurement.

Today, as an idiom, *marked man* (or *woman*) is used figuratively to signify being in danger or targeted by another as the subject of suspicion or enmity. Examples of usage include (1) Angel knew she was a marked woman when her dad learned that she had driven the family car without permission; (2) He knew he was a marked man when his confidential remarks about his boss were printed in the paper; and (3) When Adam testified in court about a mugging he had witnessed, he feared the defendant's cronies would make him a marked man.

What Is the Origin of the Distress Signal *Mayday*?

Mayday is an international radiotelephone signal used by an aircraft or ship in grave and imminent danger. Such craft are in immediate and desperate need of help. *Mayday* is an anglicized term taken from the French *m'aidez*, meaning, "help me," or *m'aider*, "to render help to me." The term *pan-pan* is another distress signal used when urgent help is needed, but it does not rise to the level of *mayday*. *Pan-pan* comes from the French word *panne*, meaning "breakdown," and is also used to communicate "man overboard."

Both *mayday* and *pan-pan* are communicated in sets of three, for example, "mayday—mayday—mayday," as part of a communication sequence. *Mayday* was first used by Frederick Stanley Mockford in 1923, and was approved as an official distress signal in 1927 at the International Radiotelegraph Convention in Washington, DC.

What Is the Origin of *OK*?

OK—also spelled *ok*, *O.K.*, *okay*, and *okeh*—serves as a succinct and universally understood indication of approval, well-being, or understanding. *OK* is distinctly an Americanism that has now spread to many other countries and cultures.

Although many theories abound regarding the origin of *OK*, the most likely involves a popular practice in Boston newspapers in the early 1800s. According to Allen Walker Read (1906–2002), American etymologist and professor at Columbia University, it was fashionable at that time to use *initialisms*, a type of abbreviation where the first letter of each word is used to indicate an expression. To assist the reader, the meaning of the initials typically followed them. Eerily like contemporary texting, examples include R.T.B.S. (remains to be seen) and T.B.F.T.B. (too big for their britches). Thinking themselves very clever, news writers considered all this quite humorous and extended the practice to the intentional misspelling of these sorts of abbreviations. A prime example was use of

O.K. for "all correct," where the words and initials do not match. It first appeared in print in March 1839.

Most of these initialisms faded into obscurity. *OK* would likely have suffered the same fate had it not been for the 1840 presidential campaign slogan of Martin Van Buren. From Kinderhook, New York, Van Buren was nicknamed "Old Kinderhook," which was abbreviated "O.K.," with his campaign linking O.K. (for *Old Kinderhook*) to OK (for *all correct*). Van Buren lost the election, but the term *OK* was permanently cemented in the language.

What Is the Origin of the Term *Oodles*?

Oodles is a fun word signifying a large amount or great number of something. Synonyms include similarly imprecise words such as *zillion*, *heap*, *passel*, or *slew*. One can have oodles of money, oodles of time, oodles of friends, oodles of ideas, and the like.

Most sources indicate that *oodles* is American English, but otherwise of uncertain origin. Its usage can be traced to 1869 and the *Overland Monthly*, a defunct literary magazine, in its quote "A Texan never has a great quantity of anything, but he has 'scads' of it, or oodles, or dead oodles, or scadoodles, or swads." It is speculated that oodles may be a corruption, contraction, or division of *the whole boodle, scadoodle, caboodle* (of *kit and caboodle*), or even *huddle*.

In pop culture, some readers may recall *Oodles* baby dolls from the 1980s. They were small, plastic, kewpie-like dolls of varying skin tones whose hair was fashioned into a closed loop so that owners could wear them as charms, pendants, or zipper pulls. *Oodles* was the name, also, of a heavy-set criminal, first introduced in 1955, in the famed comic strip, *Dick Tracy*. It was slang for *money* in Australia in the 1940s.

Arguably the most widely known usage of *oodles* today is *oodles of noodles*, a phrase popularized by Nissin Foods' Top Ramen noodles because the phrase *oodles of noodles* is featured prominently on the package.

What Is the Origin of *Waiting for the Other Shoe to Drop?*

Waiting for the other shoe to drop (or *fall*), is an American phrase that means to wait for an expected or inevitable event to occur, often negative. This idiomatic phrase dates to the early 1900s and is probably taken from life in boarding or rooming houses. *Waiting for the other shoe to drop* invokes the image of a man returning to his rented room late after work. Sitting on his spartan bed, he pulls off a shoe, letting it drop to the floor. Realizing the loud thud has certainly been heard by his neighbors, he removes his second shoe and places it carefully and quietly on the floor. Elsewhere in the boarding house, residents who heard the first shoe hit the floor develop a sense of expectation and cannot drift back to sleep because they are waiting for the other shoe to drop.

Contemporary examples of usage include (1) With the housing economy in its current state, investors are waiting for the stock market to be the other shoe to drop; and (2) Jessica waited for the other shoe to drop when she was told her boyfriend had been phoning her best friend, Annie.

What Is a Pastiche?

Pastiche (pas-teesh) can have several meanings. Most often it refers to an artistic work that openly imitates an earlier work in a flattering way or takes its inspiration from several such works. It can also mean something formed from a combination of different parts or sources—a medley of several parts, ingredients, or ideas. *Pastiche* is a French word taken from the Italian *pasticcio* (a type of pie made of an assortment of ingredients).

Examples of usage include (1) Many consider George Lucas's *Star Wars* films to be a pastiche of early science-fiction television and radio shows; (2) The architect planned the new office building to be a pastiche of the styles of Frank Lloyd Wright and Albert Kahn; and (3) The doctoral student created a presentation that was a pastiche of the content in several important pedagogy textbooks.

Synonyms for *pastiche* include *patchwork*, *collection*, *hodge-podge*, *potpourri*, *compilation*, *synthesis*, and *miscellany*, depending on the intent of the writer or speaker.

How Did the Penknife Get Its Name?

The quill pen was an important and widely used writing instrument for over one thousand years. Made from a bird feather, typically goose, quills lasted only about one week, depending on the amount of use. Other types of feathers were also used based on availability, expense, and favored type of font.

Feathers plucked from live birds were preferred; the feathers were then treated and cured. This preparation concluded with the use of a sharp cutting tool to shape the feather's shaft into a suitable writing point, then making a small slit in the tip to accommodate a small amount of ink. The cutting tool used to do this was called a *penknife* (also *pen-knife* or *pen knife*). Despite the fact that quill pens have become obsolete, the word *penknife* is still used today for a small, single-blade pocketknife.

What Is the Origin of the Phrase *Playing Hooky*?

Playing hooky (sometimes spelled *hookey* or *hookie*) is an Americanism that has existed in print from at least the mid-1800s. A common term among schoolboys, it was used, for example, by Mark Twain in *The Adventures of Tom Sawyer* (1876): "He moped to school gloomy and sad, and took his flogging, along with Joe Harper, for playing hookey the day before." A particularly popular term in New York, its usage corresponds roughly with that state's issuance of compulsory attendance laws.

There are several possible origins of this Americanism—most of them rooted in some form of dishonesty. One explanation of the phrase's origin derives from the phrase *to hook something*, an old saying for stealing, or *hooky-crooky*, also meaning dishonesty or thievery. The latter phrase gave rise to the phrase *by hook or by crook*, a phrase still used today indicating accomplishing something by any means or way possible. *Hook [it]* has also been used as slang meaning "to escape or run away." A third origin involves the Dutch term *hoekje spelen*, originally meaning the children's game of hide and seek. This source helps explain the idiom *playing hooky*, for obvious reasons.

The idiom *playing hooky* has largely been replaced by today's youth who now say they are *cutting*, *skipping*, or *ditching* school. However, the practice of playing hooky endures among kids who intentionally miss class and among adults who miss work for less-than-honest reasons.

What Are Portmanteau Words?

A portmanteau word is a made-up word constructed by combining or blending two or more separate words, sounds, or parts of words. The plural is *portmanteaux*, or *portmanteaus*, according to Merriam-Webster. As the English language evolves, portmanteaux serve a valuable function of describing new phenomena, ideas, innovations, and the like. Examples include *smog* (*smoke* + *fog*); *emoticon* (*emotion* + *icon*); *infomercial* (*information* + *commercial*); *seascape* (*sea* + *landscape*); *palimony* (*partner* + *alimony*); *blog* (*web* + *log*); and *brunch* (*breakfast* + *lunch*). Pop culture also uses this same concept for peoples' names, for example, *Brangelina* (*Brad Pitt* + *Angelina Jolie*).

First used in the late 1500s, *portmanteau* is taken from the French for "clothes rack" or "bag" (*porter* [to carry] + *manteau* [a cloak or mantle]). A portmanteau was (and is) a travel bag usually divided into two compartments. Famed writer and mathematician

Lewis Carroll introduced and popularized this term in its current usage in 1872 in *Through the Looking Glass, and What Alice Found There*. Referring to the word *slithy* (*lithe* + *slimy*), Carroll stated, "You see it's like a portmanteau—there are two meanings packed up into one word."

What Is Meant by *Pushing the Envelope*?

To push the envelope means to do something to its maximum or to exceed limits. The original phrase, *pushing the edge of the envelope*, is an aviation expression first used by post–World War II test pilots. The "envelope" referred to the parameters of what was considered safe to fly. Therefore, *pushing the envelope* was the testing and redefinition of those limits. This idiom was popularized in Tom Wolfe's 1979 book *The Right Stuff* chronicling Chuck Yeager's achievement of breaking the sound barrier and NASA's early manned spacecraft efforts; in time, it was generalized to indicate the testing of just about any limits.

Examples of usage include (1) You really are pushing the envelope young man! What do you mean by coming late to work twice this week? (2) Jenna knew she was pushing the envelope by wearing such a daring skirt to school; and (3) Jeremy was fearful of handling insects, but he knew he'd have to push the envelope if he was to achieve his dream of becoming an entomologist.

What Is Meant by *Quotidian*?

Quotidian (kwoh-tid-ee-uhn) is an adjective meaning "daily, routine, customary, trivial, or commonplace." In medicine, it refers to a fever or other symptom that occurs on a daily or regular basis. Taken from the Latin *quotidianus* (daily), this word came into English use around 1340.

Examples of usage include (1) XM Radio makes my quotidian commute to Los Angeles bearable; (2) Critics panned the artist's exhibition, calling his work quotidian at best; and (3) Shirley's quotidian headaches took a toll on the quality of her work.

What Is the Origin of the Phrase *Raining Cats and Dogs?*

Raining cats and dogs is an idiom—an expression or phrase made up of several words that has a meaning quite different than you would guess simply through analyzing the words that make up the phrase.

Raining cats and dogs, for example, is used to indicate a weather condition where it rains heavily and steadily. The most likely explanation of its origin involves the nature of poorly constructed city streets in Britain in the 1600s. A heavy rain could quickly result in a river of flowing sewage and trash. This was often a death trap for cats and dogs caught out in the deluge; when the rains subsided, their corpses were found all about the streets. Looking like they "came from the skies," the idiom came into being as a way to signify a torrential rain.

An example of this idiom's usage is "I need to put an umbrella in my backpack because the weather forecasters are calling for it to rain cats and dogs today."

What Is the Origin of the Phrase *Caught Red Handed?*

The phrase *caught red handed* (often *redhanded* or *red-handed*) means to be caught in the act of committing some misdeed or crime or to be faced with overwhelming evidence of such. Originally a legal term, *redhand* dates to the early 1400s and the reign of James I and the Scottish Acts of Parliament. It was often used in various legal documents of the day and was a direct and straightforward association with having blood on one's hands, either human through murder or animal through poaching. *Red handed* appeared in literature in the 1800s in Sir Walter Scott's *Ivanhoe*. Scott is generally credited with popularizing the phrase. In time, the literal meaning of *red handed* evolved into an idiom indicating being found out regarding any type of misdeed.

Contemporary examples of usage include (1) Garrett knew he was in big trouble when he was caught red handed taking money from his father's wallet; (2) When the trail of evidence led directly to the couple's garage, the murderers knew they had been caught red handed and would be convicted; and (3) I knew I had been caught red handed when my mom found the empty cookie jar in the kitchen and cookie crumbs on my bed.

What Is Riffraff?

Riffraff (also spelled *riff-raff*) is a disparaging term used to refer to a person or group of persons deemed disreputable, useless, or of low social standing.

Riffraff is taken from the fifteenth-century Old French *rif et raf*, shortened from *rifler* (to plunder, spoil, or strip) and *rafle* (to ravage or to carry off). This originated in reference to those in medieval times who would visit battlefields to remove any articles of worth from fallen soldiers. The phrase evolved as it moved into the Old English to mean "every little scrap," then softened in meaning to signify "one and all, everybody" then "common people."

Examples of usage include (1) My mother wouldn't let me date Jack, saying that he was riffraff; (2) The art festival charged a steep entry fee to keep the riffraff from attending; and (3) Stung by being called riffraff while in grade school, Joe made every effort in life to elevate himself through education and associating only with trustworthy, upright people.

Why Do We Use the Expression *Rule of Thumb*?

The most probable origin of the phrase *rule of thumb* involves a measurement increment guided by the length of the first joint of the thumb—approximately one inch. In this case, *rule* is associated with a ruler (an instrument of measurement), and not with a guide to conduct, like the rules of the road or school rules. The phrase *rule of thumb* is primarily credited to woodworkers and carpenters. Other "body part measurements" include a person's foot equaling what we refer to today as a *foot measurement*. We still use *hands* to indicate horse size, as another example. Naturally, thumb sizes vary, as do feet and hands. Therefore, when we say *rule of thumb*, we refer to an approximation or some type of procedure that comes more from experience than formal training.

Other explanations for the origin of this phrase do exist. The most widespread, albeit uncorroborated, explanation is associated with a British judge, Sir Francis Buller (1746–1800). Widely considered to be harsh and hasty in judgment, he is credited with a ruling that a wife could be disciplined by use of a rod that was no greater in circumference than one's thumb; he was caricatured in the press as *Judge Thumb*. As the phrase *rule of thumb* is well

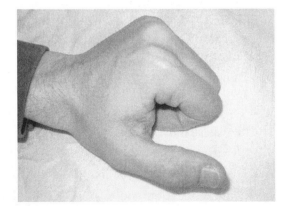

documented in print in the seventeenth century, well before the birth of Judge Buller, this attribution is considered false. Also, it is equally unlikely that the phrase was originated by brewers using their thumbs to test for proper fermentation temperature as the thumb is not sensitive enough to detect the small temperature range needed for this process.

Examples of contemporary usage include (1) Treating guests as you would like to be treated is a good rule of thumb for hosts; and (2) As a rule of thumb, take only one or two slices of meat when the platter is passed to you.

What Is Sanskrit?

Sanskrit is often called the mother of all languages and is the classical and sacred language of India and the religions of Hinduism, Buddhism, and Jainism. It is considered the oldest known language in human history, dating back at least three thousand years. The *Rigveda*, a collection of more than one thousand Hindu hymns, is the oldest known text in Sanskrit, believed to be from the second millennium BC. Used for scientific and religious dialogue, Sanskrit is widely lauded for its clarity and beauty. The word *Sanskrit* means "refined," "consecrated," or "produced in perfect form."

After the eleventh century, the use of Sanskrit declined due to the competition from other languages and the perception that it was a language only for the scholarly or wealthy. During British rule in India, Sir William Jones, a judge stationed in India in 1780, committed to learning Sanskrit and recognized the similarities between Sanskrit, Greek, and Latin. After considerable study, he suggested that Sanskrit had originated from a source shared with Latin and Greek, asserting that Sanskrit was "more perfect than the Greek, more copious than the Latin, and more exquisitely refined than either." He further noted that the similarities in vocabulary and structure could not be explained as a mere accident. This was an astounding assertion as it was widely believed that Hebrew was the foundational language for Greek and Latin. This declaration formed the foundation for a comparative study of these and other languages, resulting in what are called today *Indo-European languages*.

Sanskrit is largely considered a dead language today, but it is still used ceremonially in India and is recognized as one of India's twenty-two languages. In addition, a movement is underway in India to revive spoken and written Sanskrit. Many universities worldwide offer courses in this language.

What Is Meant by Being *Sartorial*?

Sartorial (sahr-tor-ih-uhl) is an adjective associated with stylish or well-tailored clothing, but it has been generalized somewhat to refer to anything related to one's garb or manner of dress. Used originally to refer to menswear, it may now equally apply to women's clothing. *Sartorial* came into usage in the English language in the early 1800s and was taken from the Medieval Latin *sartor*, meaning "one who patches or mends."

Examples of contemporary usage include (1) Liam, wearing his first tuxedo, admired his sartorial image in the mirror with delight; (2) I questioned her sartorial judgment when I saw her new outfit; (3) *GQ*, the magazine for male fashionistas, is replete with images of sartorial elegance; and (4) Her sartorial signature was that of a baggy t-shirt and torn jeans.

As an aside, the *sartorius* is a long, narrow muscle in the thigh that runs from the hip to the inner side of the tibia (shinbone). It is the longest muscle in the human body and was so named presumably in observance of the cross-legged sitting position tailors of yesteryear assumed in conducting their craft.

In Terms of Time, What Is a Score?

A score is twenty of something and is often used to signify time. Like *dozen*, it is a word that describes a specific number. *Score* comes from the Old English word *scoren* or *scoru*, which was taken from the Norse *skor*, a word meaning a heavy mark or notch cut in a stick for tallying or accounting purposes.

Score is often used in multiples, for example, *four score*. An iconic illustration of this usage is from Abraham Lincoln's Gettysburg Address: "Four score and seven years ago our fathers brought forth . . ." Doing the math, "four score and seven years" is 87 years ($[4 \times 20] + 7 = 87$).

What Is Meant by *Having One's Sea Legs*?

Dating to the days of sailing ship supremacy, *sea legs* first appeared in Woodes Rogers's 1712 travelogue, *A Cruising Voyage Round the World*. Its original meaning involved novice sailors becoming able to walk steadily on a ship in stormy weather or rough seas. Although still a useful nautical phrase, by the 1800s its usage broadened to indicate adjustment to a new, challenging, or difficult situation.

Examples of usage include (1) Although Lilly was stunned with the diagnosis, she began to get her sea legs by reading everything she could on lupus; and (2) Utilizing his strong study skills and ability to make new friends quickly, it didn't take Ralph long to get his sea legs in college.

What Is the Origin and Meaning of the Word *Serendipity*?

Serendipity is the good fortune of discovering something valuable or pleasing when you are not looking for it. It is the act of being fortunate by accident—pure good luck. However, it also encompasses the discoverer having the wherewithal to recognize or grasp the importance of what has been stumbled upon. Examples of serendipity include the discovery of penicillin, aspartame, x-rays, and Velcro. Serendipity can also apply to more mundane findings such as going to an interview for a job and being asked to take another (and better!) position. Another simple example is finding an interesting website when actually searching for something else on the Internet.

Serendipity as a word was first used by the English writer Horace Walpole in 1754 in a letter to Horace Mann, famed educator. In this letter, he referred to a Persian fairy tale called "The Three Princes of Serendip." Serendip was the island we now call Sri Lanka. Based on the life of Persian King Bahram V, this tale tells of three princes, all quite intelligent, setting sail for Serendip. There on the island, they make many splendid and astonishing discoveries and receive a number of unsought rewards.

What Is a Shylock?

Shylock is the hardhearted Jewish money lender in Shakespeare's *The Merchant of Venice*. Shylock, a merciless and a cruel miser, is depicted as a villain the audience "loves to hate." Controversy still exists over Shakespeare's casting of Shylock, particularly the inclusion of the scene where Shylock is duped into a forced conversion to Christianity, and the tangle of suggested anti-Semitic and anti-Christian sentiments throughout the play. Shylock's depiction has varied over the centuries, ranging from that of villain to victim to tragic hero, depending on the production.

By extension, *shylock* (lower case) today is a synonym for *loan shark*; that is, one who illegally lends money at an outrageously high, if not extortionate, rate of interest. However, using *shylock* in this or any other way has become increasingly offensive due to its linkage to possible anti-Semitic implications and the perpetuation of negative stereotypes. For these reasons, *shylock*, common in many legal statutes and codes, has been or is being eliminated from these texts.

What Is the Origin of *Blown to Smithereens*?

A smithereen is a splintered or fractured piece or bit of something. The term is first found in print in 1829 spelled as *smiddereens*. Used almost exclusively in plural form, it is almost certainly taken from the Gaelic (Irish) *smidirîn* translated as "small bit or fragment." To blow something to smithereens usually implies some sort of blast or explosion.

Examples of *smithereens* usage include (1) When I dropped the pitcher, it smashed to smithereens; (2) The Navy blew a dysfunctional spy satellite to smithereens with a three-stage missile fired from the USS *Lake Erie*; (3) Her self-esteem shattered to smithereens when she failed her entrance exam for the third time; and (4) The razing of the dormitory made it look like it had been blown to smithereens.

What Is Meant by *Snark*?

Part of the beauty of the English language is its perpetual evolution. One of the newer entries in our general usage lexicon is *snark*. The word itself is not new. First used by Lewis Carroll to name a fictional animal in his poem "The Hunting of the Snark: An Agony in Eight Fits" (1876), it has been used over the years in varying ways (it was the name of Jack London's yacht, for example) and to name various things such as a type of graph, a cruise missile, and a computer game.

Interestingly, in Britain this word came into being in the early 1900s meaning "to nag, find fault with, or nitpick"—probably from the Dutch and low German *snorken*. In America, it most often is considered a portmanteau word formed from *snide* and *remark*. Snarking is arguably best known for its use on the Internet where people make unkind, if not distressing, remarks about others in the Internet's anonymous environment. However, it has been generalized in usage to mean any sarcastic, mean-spirited, or otherwise derisive statement about another. It can also take the form of *snarky* and *snarkily*.

Examples of current usage include (1) Ever playing the snark, the professor's assessment of Janet's essay was cruel; (2) You should be ashamed of yourself for making those snarky remarks about Mary Beth; and (3) "Your point of view is laced equally with ignorance and arrogance," she snarkily replied.

What Does the Signal SOS Mean?

Wireless telegraphy using Morse code was a conventional form of communication in the early 1900s before the advent of modern communication technologies. It was particularly useful for ships that had little way to communicate with the shore or other ships otherwise. Morse code for SOS consists of a continuous sequence of three dots, three dashes, and three dots. This signal was adopted at the second Berlin Radiotelegraphic Conference in 1906 and ratified in 1908 as the international code designation for distress.

It is widely, yet erroneously, believed that SOS is an acronym for Save Our Ship, Save Our Souls, or Survivors On Ship. In fact, SOS does not stand for anything; it was chosen simply because it was easy to transmit.

What Is the Origin of the Phrase *Stealing One's Thunder*?

Stealing one's thunder means to take attention away from someone else by the actions of another or to use someone else's idea or work to one's own advantage. This phrase has a theatrical origin. For many centuries, the sound of thunder was simulated for stage purposes by rolling metal balls in troughs or bowls or by the shaking of thin sheet metal. John Dennis (1657–1734), English literary critic and playwright, created his own way to make this sound and used it in his 1709 tragedy, *Appius and Virginia*. The theater manager shut the play down after only a few performances due to poor attendance and replaced it with *Macbeth*. Soon thereafter, Dennis attended *Macbeth* and was allegedly angered to hear the sound of "his thunder." He purportedly jumped to his feet blaring something like, "That is my thunder, by God! The villains will not let me play my play, yet they steal my thunder!"

Examples of contemporary usage include (1) I didn't tell Jonathan that I was getting married because he was so excited about his new job and I didn't want to steal his thunder; (2) The inspiration for the gown was Annie's, but the company stole her thunder by attributing it to another better known designer; and (3) If you take my plan to the boss before it is complete, you will really steal my thunder.

What Is a Straw Poll?

A straw poll (often referred to as a straw vote) is a non-binding informal or practice vote. It gives groups the opportunity to see where members or individuals stand on an issue or preference. Originally used with small groups, straw polls have grown in popular use for larger forums. Straw polls are often used, for example, in the political process to determine the top-ranking candidate in a party locally, regionally, or nationally.

The idiomatic phrase *straw poll* has its origins in author John Selden's (1584–1654) writings: "Take a straw and throw it up into the air—you may see by that which way the wind is, which you shall not do by casting up a stone." O. Henry, renowned American author, later scoffed in *A Ruler of Men* (1907): "A straw vote only shows which way the hot air blows."

The first straw poll, as we have come to know it, was conducted by the *Harrisburg Pennsylvanian*. Newspaper representatives traveled to Delaware in July 1824 to determine presidential candidate preferences.

What Is a Swan Song?

Swan song is an idiomatic phrase used to indicate someone's final achievement or performance before retiring, making a major life change, or dying. This term is commonly used to describe a farewell tour or final performance of a celebrated actor or artist, but it is also frequently employed to describe similar acts of more common

Dave Rotigel

folks. As a term in English, *swan song* in its current usage was first recorded in the late 1800s.

Swan song is believed to have originated based on the incorrect belief that swans are non-vocal throughout their lives, but suddenly burst into song immediately prior to death. Although debunked as early as AD 77 by Pliny the Elder, the false notion of silent swans singing at their final life stage persisted, as is documented in a variety of literary works through the ages.

Examples of contemporary usage of *swan song* include (1) The Rolling Stones' swan song concert was held at London's O$_2$ Arena in 2007—but who knows! (2) I am moving to California tomorrow, so finishing this major task will be my swan song; and (3) Struck suddenly dead last week, Edgar could not have predicted his most recent play would be his swan song.

What Is the Origin of the Hunting Call *Tally-Ho*?

Tally-ho (also *tally ho*) was first attributed to William the Conqueror, an ardent hunter, after the Norman Conquest of 1066. The cry *tally-ho* is rooted in Old Norman (French) phrases such as *Taillis au*! *Taiaut*! and *Thia-hilaud à qui forherr*! This is a sampling of exclamations called out when game was flushed from a thicket. Corrupted by the British into the cry *Tallio*, *hoix*, *hark*, *forward* and other variations, the call evolved simply to *tally-ho*. Uttering *tally-ho* is now most closely associated with foxhunting, which typically involves mounted hunters using dogs to assist in the hunt.

Foxhunting is practiced today in Britain, the United States, India, Australia, France, and many other countries. However, this sport is not without controversy. It is banned in some countries or regions, with adversaries arguing that it is inhumane. In the

United States, foxhunting is regulated by the Masters of Fox-hounds Association of North America with an emphasis on the chase, not the kill (although a kill is not ruled out). To learn more about foxhunting in America and the Code of Hunting Practices governing foxhunts, visit http://www.mfha.org/docs/guidebooks/codeofhuntingpractices2008.pdf

What Is Meant by *Being Tongue-Tied*?

Tongue-tied used as an adjective dates to at least 55 BC as quoted in Cicero's *De Oratore*: "I prefer tongue-tied knowledge to ignorant loquacity." It continues to have a comparable meaning in signifying being unable or unwilling to speak or express oneself clearly or smoothly in social or business situations due to being shy, nervous, or embarrassed.

Contemporary examples of usage include (1) Jon was the most talkative boy at the lunch table, but became tongue-tied when Sara approached; (2) Jennie became quite tongue-tied when she tried to explain to her mother why she came home after curfew; and (3) I became increasingly tongue-tied when I approached the microphone to accept my award.

Interestingly, there is a medical condition called *ankyloglossia*, which is referred to in lay language as *being tongue-tied*. Humans have a thin fold of tissue in the mouth (the *lingual frenulum*), which is attached to the lower side of the tongue and the floor of the mouth. In cases where this attachment is thickened, shortened, or attached too close to the tip of the tongue, the person has trouble with feeding (especially as an infant) and with speech development as the tongue does not have freedom of movement. This condition may be outgrown or treated with surgery depending on individual circumstances and as recommended by a physician.

What Is the Origin of the Word *Tweak*?

Tweak originally meant "to pinch, pull, or nip something." The term likely came from a variant of the Middle English *twikken* (to pull sharply) or Old English *twiccian* (to pluck). It can also mean "to annoy, irritate, or make fun of someone."

With this in mind, some example usages are (1) Gardeners may tweak unwanted buds from the stems of plants; (2) Grandmothers may lovingly tweak the cheek of a grandchild; and (3) Students may tweak their teachers by offering endless alternate views on a topic.

However, a more common usage today often refers to adjusting, fine-tuning, or otherwise altering something to improve or perfect it. This usage was popularized by those in technology development when they used it to refer to someone who tinkered with computer hardware, software, programming, or performance. *Tweaking* in this regard quickly spread to the general population and is used widely in a variety of fields and applications.

Examples of this usage include (1) Marilyn tweaked her essay to the point where its original beauty was lost; and (2) The mechanic tweaked the timing until the engine hummed.

What Is a Tycoon?

Tycoon is a word used to signify or describe a top leader or some-one of considerable power, wealth, or influence. Tycoon is the English rendition of the Japanese word *taikun* meaning "great prince," the Japanese having borrowed this term from the Chinese language. Interestingly, the Japanese typically only used this term to impress foreign dignitaries, especially in reference to their Shogun, the commander-in-chief of the Japanese army.

Commander Matthew Perry introduced the term *taikun* as *tycoon* to America in the mid-1850s. Interestingly, it was first used in America as a term of endearment for Abraham Lincoln by his cabinet members and other government workers, but soon came to apply to a range of business and industry leaders.

Examples of usage include (1) Donald Trump, real-estate tycoon, is also well known for his reality show *The Apprentice*; (2) Bill Gates is known as the world's leading software tycoon; and (3) With her big raise, Anne bought new clothes as if she were a tycoon!

What Is Umble Pie?

Umbles is the term for the entrails (internal organs such as the liver, kidneys, and intestines) of a deer. Since at least fifteenth- or sixteenth-century England, venison was reserved for the gentry or the hunter's family. The umbles were given to the servants to eat, most often cooked into a pie. These pies were similar to contemporary meat pies (chicken pot pie, for example). In time, *umble pie* became a synonym for *humility* as those who ate it were considered inferior or of a lesser station in society.

Umble pie is often spelled and pronounced today as *humble pie*. When we *eat humble pie*, it means we act in a submissive, apologetic, or humbled fashion in recognition of an error committed. In short, like similar idioms, it means "to eat one's words" or "to eat crow."

Examples of this term's idiomatic use are (1) Judith almost choked on humble pie when she realized she, not her beleaguered assistant, had made the accounting error; and (2) I had to eat humble pie after I told my mother that she'd never get a part in the community play.

What Is the Origin of the Phrase *Willy-Nilly*?

Willy-nilly (wil-ee-nil-ee) has it roots in two definitions. Originally, it meant whether something was with or against one's will. The other, and more common usage now, when the term is used to modify a verb, means to perform the action of the verb in a disorganized, spontaneous, or haphazard manner. It can also mean "unwillingly." The first known recorded usage dates to 1608, purportedly as a contraction of *will ye, nill ye* and other spelling variations—*will* meaning something that one wants to do, and *nill* the opposite, or something to be avoided or done by compulsion. Shakespeare used the now-archaic versions *will he, nill he* (*Hamlet*) and *will you, nill you* (*The Taming of the Shrew*).

Examples of contemporary usage include (1) Jeff, knowing his son didn't want to go to college, packed him off willy-nilly anyway and hoped for the best; (2) Fearing for pedestrian safety, Borough Council was appalled at how citizens crossed the street in a willy-nilly fashion; and (3) His organizational style was clearly willy-nilly, as evidenced by the disorder of his desk.

What Is the Origin of the Word *Windfall*?

A windfall is an unexpected monetary gain or some other form of good fortune typically not the result of any efforts by the recipient.

The term *windfall* originated in the 1400s in England when felling trees was strictly controlled, with most felled trees being reserved for use by the Royal Navy. However, the law did allow the harvesting of wind-fallen branches or trees by commoners for burning or building. When Mother Nature provided a good wind, many benefited from the windfall. Hence, that which the wind provides due in no part to the gatherers' doing is a natural connection to the current meaning of *windfall*.

Examples of usage include (1) A long-lost uncle left me $100,000 when he died. What a windfall! (2) Finding that gasoline had dropped $1.00 per gallon was a big windfall for our tight family budget; and (3) Winning the lottery next week would be just the windfall I need to build and furnish a new home.

4

HOLIDAYS AND SPECIAL OCCASIONS

Why Is the Day after Thanksgiving Called *Black Friday*?

*B*lack Friday is the unofficial first day of the Christmas shopping season. It is erroneously tagged as the busiest and most profitable day of the year for merchandisers, when in fact, data suggest that sales volumes are heaviest on the few days before Christmas. Many retailers offer early or extended shopping hours and "doorbuster" prices on selected merchandise to attract consumers on Black Friday.

It is believed that the term *Black Friday* derives from accounting terminology. Retailers often depend on Christmas shopping to become profitable for the year—to be "in black ink" (profitable) as opposed to being "in red ink" (unprofitable). Therefore, what is meant is really Black (ink) Friday.

Historically, the term *Black Friday* has had a decidedly negative connotation for different reasons. For example, it is still used to refer to September 24, 1869, when financiers Jay Gould and James Fist made an unsuccessful attempt to corner the gold market. Their actions caused the stock exchange to fluctuate wildly, creating panic and the ruin of many investors. The term has also been used to signify other significant stock market drops and, in general, *any* Friday that is marked by calamity.

What Is Boxing Day?

Boxing Day is celebrated December 26 (or the first workday after Christmas) for the traditional purpose of providing money, gifts, or other items to the poor and needy. It is a public, or "bank," holiday typically observed in Britain, Canada, Australia, Hong Kong, Nigeria, and other European and African countries. Boxing Day appears to be associated with St. Stephen, one of the original deacons of the Christian Church, who cared for widows and the poor.

A key theory of the origin of Boxing Day dates to medieval times and involves wealthy British citizens giving their servants the day off after Christmas as a token of holiday generosity—to hopefully keep them happy and productive. This included presenting a box containing money, gifts, leftover food, or other desired items. Boxing Day, however, is often credited to Queen Victoria, who encouraged merchants to give boxes of fruit, foodstuffs, clothing, money, or other items to their employees as a token of appreciation. It may also have originated through the placing of money in church alms boxes, money that was then distributed to the needy after Christmas. Note that all these explanations involve the giving or filling of boxes, hence *Boxing Day*.

Today, Boxing Day is a day of family, food, sports, travel, and after-Christmas retail sales associated with the holiday season. However, community organizations continue to promote the day's original meaning by seeking volunteerism, donations to community thrift stores, and contributions to area food banks. It is also an occasion to provide a tip or other token of appreciation to those who provide good service throughout the year.

What Is the Holiday Cinco de Mayo?

Cinco de Mayo (sink-oh-duh-my-oh) is a holiday that honors the 1862 defeat of the French army by the Mexican militia at the Battle of Puebla. Cinco de Mayo (literally, "May 5" in Spanish) is *not* Mexico's independence day, although many people erroneously believe it to be so. Mexico's independence day is September 16 (1810).

In essence, Mexico was in deep debt to England, Spain, and France with no hope of being able to repay. Seeing the handwriting on the wall, England and Spain accepted vouchers of repayment, but France decided to fight for the debt with an eye toward expanding its land holdings and presence in North America. Remarkably and unexpectedly, the Mexicans defeated the French at the Batalla de Puebla, although out-gunned, out-manned, and out-supplied.

They won the battle, but lost the war. Napoleon III sent additional troops to capture Mexico City in order to install a relative, Archduke Ferdinand Maximilian of Austria, as ruler. However, this victory too was short-lived, with French forces withdrawing and Maximilian being executed in 1867.

Cinco de Mayo, celebrated only sporadically in Mexico, has become quite an event in the United States, particularly in locales with a large Mexican or Mexican American population. Starting in the United States as an event to promote Mexican pride, goodwill, and partnership, Cinco de Mayo quickly became a booming cultural event signifying courage and determination. It is celebrated in many communities and in schools across the nation. Music, mariachi bands, fireworks, dancing, and parades are common features in celebrating Cinco de Mayo.

What Does the *D* in *D-day* Stand For?

Every major military operation has a D-day. Arguably the most famous D-day occurred on June 6, 1944, when over 150,000 Allied soldiers stormed the shores of Normandy to secure a foothold in Nazi-occupied France. This advance was called *Operation Overlord*, but due to the fame and importance of this particular operation, *D-day* is the name most frequently heard.

Based on language in U.S. Army manuals, most historians agree that *D* simply means *day*, a coded designation used in many military operations. Similarly, H-hour designated the hour of an operation. For those planning an attack, days or hours prior to or after the time of attack were indicated with plus or minus signs, for example, one day prior to D-day would be D-1, and two days after D-day would be D+2.

The *D* and the *H* simply emphasize and differentiate the given day or hour as *the* day or hour. This was a practical procedure as a planned time of attack might be subject to a number of circumstances beyond the control of the planners, including weather, maritime conditions, and supply connections.

What Is the Origin of the Easter Bunny?

The Easter bunny is a rabbit-spirit that has become a regular and familiar part of the celebration of Easter in many households. Because rabbits have a well-deserved reputation for producing multiple litters of *kits* (baby rabbits) every year, they are a natural symbol of fertility. Connected with the pre-Christian worship of *Eostre*, the pagan goddess of spring, fertility, and rebirth, this association of rabbits and rebirth, as well as many others, merged with Christian celebrations of Easter. Although there are no known biblical associations between rabbits and the resurrection of Christ, the tradition persists.

It is believed that Dutch and German immigrants who settled in Pennsylvania in the 1700s brought the Easter bunny tradition with them. Called the *Oschter Haws* (Easter Hare), this was the rabbit that children believed laid the eggs found at Easter time. Children would build nests in their caps or bonnets for the Easter hare in anticipation of colorful eggs being left for them if they had

been "good" boys and girls. The tradition spread and in time, the nests became baskets filled with eggs made of chocolate and other confections. This is why Easter baskets today often have a chocolate bunny as their main attraction nestled in a nice, soft nest of cellophane grass!

What Is the Origin of the Easter Egg?

Easter is a religious holiday celebrating Christ's resurrection, but some of the traditions associated with Easter are likely linked to pre-Christian or pagan celebrations related to *Eostre*, the pagan goddess of spring, fertility, and rebirth. In many cultures, the egg represented "the seed of new life," or "rebirth"—so much so that the ancient Egyptians, Phoenicians, Hindus, and Persians, among others, believed that the world sprang forth from a colossal egg.

Most cultures and religions link eggs in some way to secular and sacred spring celebrations important to them as marking the emergence from winter. Folk customs and pagan traditions such as Easter eggs, Easter bunnies, and baskets filled with candy often accompany the religious aspect of the holiday. Eggs, in particular, have been adorned, painted, etched, dyed, hung from trees, rolled, hunted, exchanged, begged for, buried under buildings for luck, and included in many other traditions for millennia.

Many early Christians embraced the egg as a symbol of Christ's tomb and its promise of new life through His resurrection. So, the egg not only signified rebirth and renewal in general, but the rebirth of man. In many Christian sects, Lent, the forty-day period before Easter, prohibited the consumption of meat or meat products. Eggs, also a prohibited food, were often hardboiled and decorated in anticipation of eating them at Easter when the period of privation had ended.

Egg traditions familiar to Americans include egg hunts, where children search for candy eggs hidden in the grass, shrubs, and other areas with a goal to find as many eggs as possible. Egg rolling is another tradition, perhaps the most widely known Easter egg roll being that of the White House Easter Egg Roll. Begun by Dolley Madison in the early nineteenth century, this is a yearly event held for the nation's children twelve years old or younger; adults may attend, but only if accompanied by children. It is the only day in the year when the public is invited to walk about the White House lawn. For a recent White House Easter Egg Roll, nineteen-thousand eggs were hardboiled for hunting and rolling!

What Is Fat Tuesday?

Mardi Gras activities begin in January and terminate at midnight on Fat Tuesday with the start of Ash Wednesday—the beginning of Lent. *Mardi Gras* is French for *Fat Tuesday*, and all the activities that take place are considered a time of enjoyment and indulgence before the customary fasting, penance, and preparation for Easter associated with Lent. Fat Tuesday, once widely-known as *Shrove*

Tuesday, is celebrated by millions every year all around the world. In the United States, New Orleans is noted for its raucous celebrations replete with parades and masked balls. These activities have taken place in New Orleans since the early 1700s when French settlers arrived in the area. Much of Mardi Gras has its roots in pagan spring festivals that under Christian influence became part of Lent and Easter celebrations.

Mardi Gras is known for its spectacular celebrations ranging from street festivities open to everybody to lavish private parties. Thousands of people belong to about sixty *krewes*, or groups of people who plan parties and parades around New Orleans. Tourists and residents alike covet catching strings of beads and other tokens tossed from the parade floats.

The first modern-day type of Mardi Gras parade was organized in 1857 by the Mystik Krewe of Comus. In 1872, on the occasion of a visit to New Orleans by Russian Grand Duke Alexis Romanoff, several New Orleans citizens formed the Krewe of Rex to honor him. Ever since that time, the naming of kings and queens has been a part of the revelry. The colors of the house of Romanoff, purple (justice), green (faith), and gold (power), were adopted as the colors of Mardi Gras and remain as such today.

Why Is Flag Day Celebrated in the United States?

Flag Day is an American tradition celebrated every June 14. It commemorates and celebrates the adoption of the flag and the flag's proud history. It is also a time to learn about and show proper respect toward this national symbol. The American flag was adopted in 1777 through a resolution of the Second Continental Congress. Much of the impetus for recognizing and honoring the flag came from the nation's teachers and school children over the decades; their patriotism caught on and provided a model for others to follow and make official. It was not until 1916 that President Woodrow Wilson proclaimed June 14th Flag Day, followed in 1949 by the establishment of National Flag Day by Congress during President Truman's administration.

Perhaps the most renowned individuals associated with the flag are Betsy Ross, who sewed the country's first flag (Ross served as a seamstress for George Washington and made the flag at his request), and Francis Scott Key, who wrote the lyrics of *The Star-Spangled Banner* under harrowing conditions.

Flags of all kinds are an enduring topic of study, collection, and interest. *Vexillology* is the study of flags, and those who study them are called *vexillologists*. Taken from the Latin *vexillum*, meaning "flag," the term was first used by Whitney Smith, flag expert, in the late 1950s.

What Are the Ides of March?

The Ides of March live in historical notoriety as the day Julius Caesar was brutally assassinated by Marcus Brutus and his fellow conspirators—March 15, 44 BC. Caesar, although rebuffing the notion of becoming a king, had no such reservation about becoming dictator for life and did so in February 44 BC. This caused a great deal of suspicion and loathing among his opponents as Roman society had long rejected a royal form of government. Scholars speculate that this move likely provoked his enemies to actively plot his death—it was the final straw, so to speak. Marcus Brutus is credited with masterminding and participating in the fatal attack. Ironically, after Brutus's defeat by Caesar in Rome's most recent civil war, Caesar had spared Brutus's life and eventually promoted him to praetor, a very high-ranking position responsible for judicial matters. Caesar did this as he recognized Brutus's talent and strength—plus the fact that Brutus's mother was one of Caesar's personal companions. Both men have been portrayed as villain or redeemer over time, depending on the historical or literary source.

The Roman calendar was organized around certain regular lunar events focusing on three days: Kalends (first day of the month), Nones (fifth or seventh days of specified months), and the Ides (fifteenth day in March, May, July, and October; thirteenth day of all other months). The Ides of March was just another day. In and of itself, the Ides did not assume an air of foreboding until sixteen centuries later when Caesar's death was reenacted in Shakespeare's play (based on Plutarch) *Julius Caesar*, where the soothsayer (seer of the future) warns Caesar, "Beware the Ides of March." We no longer use this method of calendar organization, and the word *Ides* is almost exclusively evocative of Caesar's demise.

Why Do We Carve Jack-o-Lanterns at Halloween?

Jack-o-lanterns have been a part of Halloween observances for centuries. They date to the time of the Irish legend of Stingy Jack, reputedly an avid drinker and trickster. Having imbibed far too much at a pub one night, Jack, drinking with Satan, offered his soul if Satan would turn himself into a sixpence to pay for the drinks. Once Satan had done so, Jack placed the "coin" in his pocket, which held a silver cross—an object that prevented Satan from reverting to his natural form. Duped, the Devil agreed to leave Jack alone for ten years if he was allowed to be set free, which was agreed upon. Ten years later, Satan reappeared to collect Jack's soul. Asking only that the Devil climb a nearby tree to pluck a final apple for him, Jack quickly carved the sign of the cross in the trunk, which prevented Satan from climbing back down. In exchange for his freedom, the Devil agreed to *never* take Jack's soul.

Upon his death, Stingy Jack was denied entrance into heaven as he was deemed undesirable. Satan, who kept his word, also denied him entrance into the underworld, but he did give Jack a glowing ember so that he could make his way in the dark night. Since then, Jack has been consigned to wander the dark alone as a condemned soul. *Jack of the Lantern* became *Jack O'Lantern* (often spelled *jack-o-lantern*).

Once the legend of the mythical Stingy Jack spread, residents carved or painted scary faces on potatoes or turnips to keep the presence of Stingy Jack and other evil spirits from their dwellings.

With the advent of the Irish Potato Famine in the mid-1800s, waves of Irish immigrants came to America along with many of their traditions. The immigrants found that pumpkins made excellent jack-o-lanterns, and the tradition endured, with the jack-o-lantern being arguably the most widely recognized symbol of Halloween today.

Who Is Krampus?

Despite the number of American Christmas traditions originating in Europe, Krampus (sometimes spelled *Krampuss*) is typically not one of them. Krampus, according to legend, was the dark, goat-faced, demonic companion of Saint Nicholas some five hundred years ago. Krampus was so-named from the Old German word *krampen*, meaning "claw." Although several interpretations of the Christmas role of Krampus exist, perhaps the best known is that of Santa's helper who, in accordance with Santa's orders, dispensed desired presents to "good" boys and girls and switches and bad dreams to the "naughty" ones. Other legends have Krampus preceding Saint Nicholas to scare disobedient children and the wicked spirits believed to roam about the streets. Activities depicting Krampus or Krampus-like figures were widely celebrated until the time of the Inquisition when it became punishable by death to impersonate demonic images. Naturally, this discouraged such traditions.

Years later, Krampus resurfaced in European Christmas celebrations to some degree and varied in interpretation from country to country. Today, one of the best-known celebrations of the legend of Krampus is the Krampus Run held in Munich as part of the Advent calendar. During this event, young men dress in fur costumes featuring ghoulish, horned masks and race through the market—all in good fun.

What Is Sadie Hawkins Day?

Sadie Hawkins Day originated through the cartoon strip *Li'l Abner* by Al Capp in 1937. Sadie Hawkins was a character in the comic deemed ugly ("homeliest gal in the hills") and unable to attract any beaus. When Sadie reached the age of thirty-five with no prospects of marriage in sight, her father, Hekzebiah Hawkins, organized a foot race to include all the unmarried men in Dogpatch, the setting of this fictional comic. After a fair (short) head start by the men, if Sadie caught a man, matrimony would follow. The other spinsters in town, thinking this was a fine event, insisted it be held annually every November.

Interestingly, Sadie Hawkins's race became a cultural phenomenon beyond the comic strip, with the idea of role-reversal becoming quite popular in schools and on college campuses. Sadie Hawkin's dances sprang up where the girls or young women would ask boys or young men to attend as their dates. Seeing its overwhelming popularity, Capp continued the plot line of the Sadie Hawkins race for the next four decades. Sadie Hawkins dances and other similar events, although less popular now, are still held throughout the nation on the first Saturday in November on or after November 9.

Sadie Hawkins Day is not to be confused with Leap Day, February 29, the day every four years when women, according to folklore, are empowered to ask a man for his hand in marriage.

What Was the Saint Valentine's Day Massacre?

The 1920s were the time of Prohibition, with the Eighteenth Amendment to the Constitution making the manufacture, sale, or transportation of intoxicating liquor illegal (this amendment was later repealed by the Twenty-First Amendment). Due to this, unlawful acts abounded with a goal of circumventing this law.

Gambling, protection rackets, and other societal transgressions were also rampant and flourished in areas across the country. Al "Scarface" Capone (1899–1947), one of the most notorious gangsters in American history, became a mob leader by making alcohol and selling it through a network of bars called *speakeasies*. He was also suspected of involvement in many other unlawful operations.

Capone and rivals often engaged in gang wars to eradicate competition (each other!) in order to gain supremacy in Chicago's organized-crime operations. Perhaps one of the most infamous incidents along these lines occurred February 14, 1929. It is alleged that Capone initiated a plot to eliminate his chief rival, George "Bugs" Moran, by luring him and his top men to a garage where Moran stored illegal liquor. Posing as police officers, Capone's men entered the garage, disarmed Moran's workers (and one hapless visitor), lined up the seven men with their faces to a wall, and opened fire with automatic weapons. Bugs Moran, the intended target, was late to the meeting and avoided his own murder. However, his power was broken, allowing Capone to take over Chicago operations. Capone himself was in Florida at the time and no one was ever tried for this heinous crime, dubbed by the media the *Saint Valentine's Day Massacre*.

Capone has been immortalized in films, television, and song lyrics over the years as the mystique and legend of organized crime continues to entertain and fascinate. A nursing home is now built on the site where the garage once stood.

What Is the History of the Tooth Fairy?

The Tooth Fairy is well known to most young children as a small, human-like sprite that visits during the night to replace a lost baby tooth (also called a *milk tooth*) placed under the pillow with money or some other treat. Ancient lore, steeped in fear and superstition, once involved the burning of baby teeth to keep them from witches or other sorcerers; it was believed that hair, fingernail parings, or teeth could be used to place a curse on the original owner of these things. Some cultures buried baby teeth in the garden, ostensibly to assist in the proper growth of the new tooth replacing it. The Vikings were said to have paid a "tooth fee" to their children for their baby teeth and then would use the teeth to make jewelry to assure power and fortune in battle.

The Tooth Fairy as we know her today came to be in the early 1900s. The legend is believed to have sprung from the eighteenth-century French fairy tale *La Bonne Petite Souris*, a story of royalty, mice, fairies, and teeth. Popularized in a children's play by Esther Watkins Arnold (1927) called *The Tooth Fairy*, followed by Lee Rothgow's book (1949) of the same name, the practice of exchanging baby teeth for money has grown to the point where the Tooth Fairy is now a representative of sorts for good dental hygiene, the main character of a host of children's books, and the thrust behind many commercial items bearing her perceived likeness.

Why Is June Considered the Wedding Month?

June was named after Juno, the Roman goddess of marriage. In ancient times, June was devoted to elements of the heart and home matters; marrying during this period of the year was considered blessed by Juno and, therefore, provident of a happy, prosperous, and long marriage. Reinforcing this tradition, in fifteenth- and sixteenth-century Europe, May was "bath month," the month in which commoners enjoyed their yearly bath after a long, hard winter. June was the perfect month to marry as everyone was relatively clean! Many contemporary wedding traditions also persist from superstitions of yesteryear. An example of this is the bride's wearing of a veil, which was thought to provide protection against evil spirits.

June is still considered a wedding month, but August rivals it in popularity today. Marriage, it should be noted, is a serious proposition. Approximately, 90 percent of adult Americans marry, with about 50 percent of these divorcing. If divorced, 80 percent will remarry someone else, with 60 percent of these eventually divorcing.

5

HUMANITIES AND CULTURE

Why Are There Fifty-Two Cards in a Deck of Cards?

Playing cards were once luxury items owned only by royalty and those of means. Each card was hand-painted, which made them pricey indeed. Thought to have originated in China or India, playing cards first came to Europe in the 1370s most likely via merchants with Islamic Mamlūk (Egyptian) connections, among whom card playing was popular. As printing methods improved, the time and cost associated with making cards dropped dramatically. German woodblock printing gave way to French stenciling, which necessitated that suitmarks be simplified to assure legibility. French suitmarks from the 1500s are the now-familiar international symbols of spade (F. *pique*), heart (F. *coeur*), diamond (F. *carreau*), and club (F. *trefle*). The original Mamlūk suitmarks were swords, polo sticks, goblets, and coins. Cards were played as a pastime, for money, and for fortune-telling.

The French continued the Mamlūk practice of using fifty-two cards in a deck with thirteen cards per suit, which is now the international standard. It is interesting to note that there seem to be a number of similarities between the organization of a deck of cards and the calendar: twelve face cards and twelve months of the year; two colors (red and black) and two halves of the year (marked by the summer and winter solstices); four suits and four seasons; and fifty-two cards in a deck versus fifty-two weeks of the year, for example.

Today, nonstandard decks of cards are available for specific games or purposes and may range from twenty-four to sixty-four individual cards each. Jokers, an American inspiration, were added in the mid-nineteenth century for playing euchre and are now used in poker, rummy, and other games as needed.

Why Is the Academy Awards Statuette Called *Oscar*?

The Academy of Motion Picture Arts and Sciences was incorporated in 1927. One of the goals of the organization was to recognize excellence in various areas of filmmaking. The first awards banquet was held on May 16, 1929, and featured the awarding of fifteen trophies (simply called *statuettes* at the time). The origin of the name *Oscar* is unclear, but it is attributed to the Academy's librarian and, later, executive director, Margaret Herrick, who commented that the statuette reminded her of her Uncle Oscar. The statuette is officially named the Academy Award of Merit, but the Academy itself typically refers to it as *Oscar*, and has done so since 1939.

Each Oscar is 13.5 inches tall and weighs 8.5 pounds. The statuette itself depicts a knight holding a sword standing on a reel of film. Made by Chicago-based R. S. Owens & Company, the Oscars are cast in brittania, a metal alloy, which is then plated in layers of copper, nickel, silver, and, finally, 24-karat gold. Since the first Academy Awards, approximately three thousand Oscars have been presented, the first going to Emil Jannings for best actor.

What Is the Proper Protocol for Addressing Present and Former U.S. Presidents?

For those fortunate enough to converse with a sitting president, the correct address would be *Mr. President* or *Sir*, and never by surname, such as *Mr. Obama*. The surname is also not used if introducing the president to another person; he is addressed as *the President* or *the President of the United States*. According to the *Associated Press Stylebook* (2009), the now correct etiquette in writing a president's name is to use the sequence of title–first name–surname, such as *President Barack Obama* or *former President Bill Clinton* as a first reference, then the surname only for subsequent references.

Once a president leaves office, it is considered most correct to address him as Mr., for example, Mr. Bush or Mr. Carter. If another title exists that indicates his highest title prior to the presidency, such as *General*, *Senator*, or *Governor*, this may be used. However, as a courtesy, we often hear former presidents called *Mr. President* or *President* [surname] when interviewed or otherwise addressed.

That said, it is not uncommon, however, for the media or others to use variations of any of these protocols, which can cause confusion for the public. For example, when we hear the use of *Governor Huckabee* or *Governor Rendell*, there is no indication of the "former" status of the title of either individual, and one might presume that the person addressed as such is still an officeholder.

Why Do We Swear by Alexander's Beard?

Alexander the Great (356–323 BC), king of Macedonia, preferred to be clean-shaven at all times. This was a marked departure from the trend of the day as beards were considered symbolic of wisdom and dignity. Alexander considered facial hair to be dangerous in time of battle, fearing it provided the enemy an easy grasp.

To refer to Alexander's beard is to refer to something that does not exist, so when we swear by Alexander's beard, we are swearing by nothing at all. An example of contemporary usage: I could have accepted his innocence if he had sworn on his mother's grave, but the fact that he swore by Alexander's beard made me immediately suspicious.

Who Was Annie Oakley?

Phoebe Ann Mozee (1860–1926) was a legendary markswoman with a variety of firearms—pistol, shotgun, and rifle. Born in Ohio, she was the fifth of seven children. Her childhood was punctuated by the death of her father, time on a county poor farm, mistreatment, injury, and other maladies. To help support her family, she hunted and sold small game. By the age of fifteen, she was so successful she was able to save the family farm by paying off the $200 mortgage. Her shooting reputation earned her an invitation to participate in a shooting contest against Frank E. Butler, a noted marksman of the day. She won the contest and his heart—Oakley and Butler were married about a year later. Her family name is often reported as Moses or Mosey, but Annie used Mozee until she adopted the stage name of Oakley, reportedly from the name of a town in Ohio; she was Mrs. Frank Butler in all other matters.

Standing a full five feet in height, Oakley was called "Little Sure Shot" by Chief Sitting Bull and gained widespread fame as a star attraction in Buffalo Bill's Wild West Show, which toured in America and Europe. Oakley, an ambidextrous shot of unerring accuracy, earned an impressive array of medals, trophies, and awards for her superior skills. She was generous in fundraising for various charities and the war effort (WWI), often gave away tickets to her show, and coached thousands of women in firearm use free of charge. Oakley was her own woman, and although she did not align herself with the feminist movements of the day, she did provide a powerful role model for women who wanted to expand their horizons.

Oakley led an active and exciting life even in retirement. Although she had never lived in the West, she was clearly a Western folk hero in her day and has been immortalized by numerous stage and film productions chronicling her accomplishments, perhaps most notably, the musical *Annie Get Your Gun*. She and her husband died of natural causes in November 1926, eighteen days apart.

Why Have Students Traditionally Given an Apple as a Gift to Teachers?

Although the origin of the relationship between apples and teachers is unclear, school children have presented their teachers with apples or apple-oriented gifts for decades. The custom also exists in other countries, notably Denmark and Sweden. Some believe that the practice of presenting a shiny, fresh apple to a teacher was a way to share abundant produce; others believe it was a way for the community to supplement the income of grossly underpaid teachers.

However, the most prevalent and logical explanation is the connection between students and their attempts to curry favor with the teacher. This practice gave rise in the 1920s to the still-used

phrase *apple-polisher*, which is synonymous with other unflattering descriptors such as *sycophant, bootlicker,* and *toady. Apple for the teacher*, particularly in the business world, is now often roughly translated as "a bribe."

Despite all this, in the world of education, giving an apple to a teacher is mostly seen as a simple, traditional, uncorrupted expression of appreciation, or as a symbol for teaching, teachers, or education. In fact, teachers often decorate their classrooms with an apple motif.

What Is Asphalt?

Asphalt is the shortened version of the term *asphalt cement*. It is a liquid or semisolid material that occurs naturally as hydrocarbons called *bitumen*. The overwhelming majority of asphalt today is produced through the process of refining oil. After other products such as naphtha, paraffin, lubricating oil, diesel fuel, gasoline, and kerosene have been removed, the remaining residue is asphalt. It is typically dark brown to black in color with a chemical content that varies depending on the source of the oil.

Asphalt has been used for building, sealing, and preservative purposes since at least 6000 BC. Its name is derived from the Late Latin *asphaltus*, taken from the Greek *ásphaltos*. Asphalt, when mixed with sand or crushed rock, is a proven contemporary construction material for roadways, airport runways, walkways, tennis courts, roofs, and waterproofing applications.

What Is Meant by *Balkanization*?

Balkanization is a term that came into being in the early twentieth century and refers to the political division of the Balkan States (Balkan Peninsula) into smaller, discordant nations after World War I.

This involved the European section of the former Ottoman Empire, a region of the world that has frequently experienced military, ethnic, and political conflict.

Balkanization (often written with a lowercase *B* as *balkanization*) has come to mean the compartmentalization or division of any entity into smaller, usually weaker, units. Examples of usage include (1) Some citizens fear that bilingual education will contribute to a balkanized American identity; and (2) The couple had such small amounts of money saved in so many accounts, they risked financial balkanization.

Why Are Barns Painted Red?

Not all barns are painted red, but red is certainly considered the most traditional color. Keep in mind that there was no such thing as purchasing ready-mixed paint until relatively recently; farmers of yesteryear had to make their own paint.

European farmers often mixed linseed oil with a combination of milk, lime (CaO), and turpentine to make paint. American farmers

Richard S. "Chip" Russell

improved this recipe by adding a substance often readily available in the soil—iron oxide, or rust (Fe_2O_3). Iron oxide retarded the growth of moss, fungi, and other moisture-trapping flora, which often rotted wooden barns. In addition, the dark red color absorbed sunlight and helped keep the barn warmer for livestock.

Due to its affordability, utility, and plastic-like properties when dry, this type of paint became increasingly popular as it was both functional and affordable. Red barns became the norm. Today, even using commercial paints, there are still many red barns, but it is not uncommon to see a barn of almost any color.

Who Was and What Is a Beau Brummell?

George Bryan "Beau" Brummell (1778–1840) is best known as a trendsetter and authority on men's fashion during the Regency Period in English history. A commoner by birth, Brummell was exposed to aristocratic life through his father who served as Lord North's private secretary. Lord North served as prime minister for George III; both men played pivotal roles in the American Revolution.

Brummell was a friend of the Prince Regent (Prince of Wales, the future George IV). It is said that at the age of twenty-one, the prince, also interested in high fashion, attended his first session in the House of Lords dressed in pink high heels and a velvet jacket lined in pink satin trimmed with gold embroidery. Brummell's style, however, was more tailored, favoring a fine cut, quality fabrics, simple lines, and elaborately-tied neckwear. He is credited with popularizing the wearing of trousers rather than the then-fashionable knee breeches, and he is credited with the introduction of a front cutaway-styled jacket with tails. In addition, he popularized the wearing of clean clothing on a clean body! Brummell enjoyed success and influence as the prince's close friend and revolutionized style throughout the England.

Brummell's high living and penchant for gambling, however, quickly depleted his bank account, and he was no longer able to live his high society life. This, coupled with a more devastating blow—the loss of his friendship with the prince—resulted in his fleeing to France to avoid debtor's prison. Brummell died a pauper in a French asylum for the insane.

Brummell's sartorial reputation did not succumb with him; his fashion sense still greatly influences menswear today. In addition, Beau Brummel (spelled with one *L*) is the name of a popular company based in New York City known for its quality, elegant, upscale menswear. The term *Beau Brummell* today is used to describe a well-dressed man, for example, "When he picked me up for our date, I loved his look—a real *Beau Brummell.*"

What Is a Blog?

A blog (blawg) is a personal or organizational journal posted online. It may be open to the public or available only to invited readers. An international phenomenon, the blog is often a mixture of personal commentary, recommended websites, and other postings. *Blog* is a portmanteau word composed of *web* and *log*. Updated frequently, often daily, blogs are formatted in a reverse chronological sequence: the last entry comes first. Blogs can range from forums for personal thoughts to newsletters to more serious and factual content, such as news and education. They can focus on conventional or traditional topics, special interests, or controversial topics. Families can even set up blog sites so that relatives can stay in touch. Blogs are considered by many to be the ultimate forum for public expression and information transmission.

Most blogs take on the personality and intent of the author(s); some blogs are syndicated to subscribers; some blogs are set up to accept feedback from others. Given the conservative estimate that a minimum of 55 million blog sites are available online, the topics of blogs and the quality with which they are written can vary widely. Due to this glut of information, blog search engines (i.e., Google Blog Search) exist to help narrow searches and locate suitable sites. Not surprisingly, those who blog are called *bloggers*, and the world of blogs is referred to as the *blogosphere*.

What Are Blue Laws?

Blue laws are ordinances designed to control commerce or limit the hours of business on Sunday. The often underlying purpose of blue laws is to promote "proper" activities or behaviors. Blue law history began in America in 1656 when settlers in New Haven, Connecticut, were given a set of laws to follow aimed at keeping the Sabbath holy. Based on Puritanical thinking, the laws provided that infractions be dealt with severely through the use of fines, the pillory or stocks, whippings, and dismemberment.

The term *blue laws* was not used until 1781, however, when Reverend Samuel Peters penned his book *General History of Connecticut*, he referred to the above laws as "blue laws." The origin of the term is unclear, but it is thought that *blue* was used in a pejorative sense for someone who was morally or otherwise rigid; for example,

this type of person may be referred to as a *bluenose*. It is often reported that the original laws were written on blue paper (hence *blue* laws), but no evidence exists to support this assertion.

Numerous court cases have been filed since the 1850s related to blue laws, but the U.S. Supreme Court has ruled that these laws are legal, constitutional, and do not violate the First Amendment if they can be demonstrated to have a secular purpose.

What Is the Origin of the Term *Busboy*?

A busboy (now called a *busperson*) is a male or female who sets and clears tables in a restaurant and performs other tasks as required by restaurant staff. First in use around 1913, it is likely that *bus* is an abbreviation of the Latin *omnibus* meaning "for all." A busperson typically conducts his or her work from a cart called a *bus*. This is a dual reference to the many and varied tasks of a busperson (*omnibus* duties) and the resemblance of their scurrying to-and-fro with their four-wheeled cart to the travels of a city bus. Many people have held the job of busperson during the span of their lives. Some particularly famous ones include Alec Baldwin (actor), Raymond Orteig (hotel magnate), and Jon Stewart (comedian).

Examples of usage of these terms include (1) When you eat at a fast food restaurant, you are expected to bus your own table; (2) I bused [or bussed] tables in college just to make enough money to buy my textbooks; and (3) Although some think my job as a busperson is demeaning, I say there is no shame in any job well done.

Why Don't Trains Have Cabooses Anymore?

All trains used to have an end or last car called a *caboose*. This car was where the conductor, brakeman, or other crew rode to conduct their work without interfering with the passengers (or the passengers interfering with them!). The caboose had side windows and a roof hatch or cupola that allowed the brakeman an opportunity to visually detect problems such as smoke from the brakes or problems with the track ahead. Typically painted red for visibility, the caboose was used as a bunkhouse, office, and kitchen for the crew. The crew often called the caboose by nicknames such as *shack*, *bobber*, and *hack*. *Caboose* itself is a word of nautical origin referring to an area on the deck of a ship where cooking took place.

All U.S. trains were required to have a caboose until the 1980s when the Flashing Rear End Device (FRED) was introduced. Also called an end-of-train device (ETD or EOT), this system provides data about the security of car couplings, the weight-load distribution, and certain hazard notifications. In short, the caboose became a victim of improved technology. Many have been sold as surplus and now serve as roadside eateries, vacation cabins, or collectibles. Cabooses are rarely put to their original use today except on repair trains or vintage trains used for exhibition or tourism.

What Is the Difference between Cement and Concrete?

The terms *concrete* and *cement* are often used interchangeably, but they mean two different things. Cement is composed primarily of limestone, calcium, silicone, iron, and aluminum. These ingredients are heated in a kiln at about 2,700 degrees until the material resembles marbles (called *clinkers*). The clinkers are then ground into a powder. Gypsum is added, and the mixture is bagged for sale in home improvement stores or for commercial use. Cement was used by the Greeks and the Romans, but when the Roman Empire fell, the use of cement all but disappeared. In fact, *cement* comes from the Latin word *caementum*. Cement was later rediscovered by Joseph Aspdin in England in the 1700s. He patented this product, calling it *Portland cement* (because he thought it resembled the limestone on England's Isle of Portland). Portland cement is a generic, not a brand, name.

Concrete, on the other hand, is cement to which aggregate (e.g., sand or gravel) and water is added. *Concrete* comes from the Latin word *concretus*. Water hydrates cement and allows it to harden, or "cure." Concrete actually becomes increasingly harder and stronger

for years after it dries. In addition, concrete can be poured around wire or rods to reinforce the concrete and make it even stronger for certain applications. Only about 10–15 percent of concrete is cement, which acts as a binder to keep the rock-like mass together.

So . . . when you walk down a sidewalk, you are walking on a concrete sidewalk, not a cement sidewalk. Likewise, when you drive over a bridge, you are driving over a concrete bridge, not a cement bridge.

What Is a Cenotaph?

A cenotaph is a monument or memorial erected to honor a deceased person or a group of persons whose remains are buried or otherwise resting elsewhere. It can also apply to a burial monument erected when the body of the deceased is unrecoverable, such as for someone lost at sea or for missing and presumed dead victims of natural or human-caused disasters.

The word *cenotaph* comes from the French *cénotaphe*, which was taken originally from the Greek for "empty tomb." A cenotaph is often built for ceremonial purposes and may be religious or secular in purpose. The erecting of cenotaphs is a practice observed around the world. Examples of several well-known cenotaphs include:

- The Hiroshima Memorial Cenotaph, Japan (to pay tribute to the atomic bomb casualties)
- The Cenotaph, London (to honor fallen World War I soldiers)
- The Vietnam Veterans Memorial, Washington, DC (to honor those who died in Vietnam)
- The Mausoleum of Genghis Khan, China (to commemorate and honor Genghis Khan's life)

⊱ The cenotaph and Ceremonial Space, Tampa, Florida
(to honor fallen Seminoles and the rightful place of the
Seminoles in Florida)

What Is a Coat of Arms?

Coats of arms first appeared in rudimentary forms in the time of
the Roman Empire around the first century. Insignia were displayed
on soldiers' shields to tell the warring factions apart. During medieval times the practice of *personal* shield insignia arose. Certain
symbols, colors, and designs on a soldier's shield signified not
only which army the soldier fought for, but often the identity of
the soldier. This was particularly useful in identifying the gravely
wounded or dead. By the fourteenth century, personal insignia began to appear on soldiers' clothing, most notably the *surcoat*, a garment worn over the armor and mail—hence the term *coat of arms*.
History is replete with occasions where individuals or groups wore
false arms to deceive the enemy or to blend in and avoid attention.

Armorial insignia on shields or banners were widespread in feu-
dal times. Because individuals, families, towns, lordships, abbeys,
and other entities were freely designing and changing their coats of
arms at will, England put a halt to the practice by founding the College of Arms, or Heralds' College of England, to register, regulate,
and control the practice in Britain as coats of arms were increasingly coming to signify inherited family and social status. Even today, the College grants coats of arms, but it is an expensive process.

What Is the Difference between a College and a University?

What may seem a simple question is more complicated than it appears. In the United States, a college is a post-secondary school

where students pursue bachelor's or associate's degrees. Colleges are typically smaller and more focused on the teaching facets of education as opposed to the research aspects. As an example, Randolph-Macon College in Ashland, Virginia, offers a variety of liberal arts undergraduate programs only (majors and minors) and, as defined above, is a college. Universities, in contrast, are typically composed of several colleges or schools—for example, Indiana University of Pennsylvania's Eberly College of Business and Information Technology, College of Education and Education Technology, College of Fine Arts, and so on. Universities characteristically offer advanced graduate degrees like master's or doctoral degrees or, in some cases, specialized professional schools for law or medicine.

Keith Boyer/IUP

However, there is nothing straightforward about these terms. Dartmouth College, Boston College, and the College of William & Mary, as examples, maintain *college* as part of their names by choice, although they are universities in every sense of the word. They do this presumably to maintain a link with their respective historical backgrounds. Likewise, *college* can also be used in the names of technical, two-year, and certificate-granting schools that do not fit the characteristics noted above. Furthermore, *institute* may be used in a university's name, such as the Massachusetts Institute of Technology (MIT). In other cases, *school* or *academy* can be used to represent a college or university.

What Is Crenellation?

Crenellation is an architectural term used to describe ramparts built around the top of a castle. Regular gaps, notches, or indentations were built in the stonework of these ramparts. The notches in the stonework were and are called *crenels* and the raised sections of stonework, *merlons*. Essentially, a soldier would stand behind a merlon and fire through a crenel with a purpose of being protected from returned fire by the merlon. A crenellated wall offered soldiers a vantage point from which to assess an impending attack and served as a warning of self-defense to any would-be attacker. A rampart of this design is called a crenellated rampart or tower.

In medieval times, Europeans were required to apply for a license to crenellate. This was not an attempt to control or regulate building, nor was it to raise funds for the monarch. Rather, it seemed to be a symbolic way to signify aristocratic status. It was common to

approve licenses for those of relatively modest means or for well-known clerics (none of whom intended or had the means to build anything resembling a castle) simply to denote a royal connection, recognition, or tribute. In short, it was a process for the socially motivated to publicly show their social rank or status.

Few are building castles these days, but *crenellation* can also refer to other architectural or decorative applications. Examples include crenellated crown molding, a row of finials or other structures installed along the top peak of a long roofline, and some fabric trims for clothing.

Who Was Croesus?

King Croesus (*kree-sus*) was the last king of Lydia and reigned from about 560–546 BC. What was the ancient kingdom of Lydia is now part of Turkey. Lydia is perhaps best known for the Pactolus, a river rich in gold deposits. King Croesus harnessed this resource and built gold refining operations, through which he minted gold coins for his kingdom. The Pactolus was one source of Croesus's great wealth.

Croesus had a fascinating life; much of what we know is a mix of fact and fiction. One tale considered to be factual was his visit to the Oracle of Delphi. An oracle was believed to consult deities for prophetic guidance. When Croesus was contemplating the invasion of Persia, the oracle told him, "You shall destroy a great nation." Croesus naturally assumed that victory would be his, when in fact, the "great nation" destroyed was his own—with a resounding defeat at the hands of the Persians!

Croesus is still renowned today for his great riches, and the phrase *rich as Croesus* continues to be a powerful and unambiguous simile for great wealth.

When Viewing a TV or Computer Monitor Shown on TV, Why Does the Picture Appear Wavy?

Older screens are cathode ray tube–based (CRT). A CRT, commonly called a *picture tube*, is a specialized vacuum tube with the inside of its screen coated with dots of chemicals called *phosphors*. At the back of the tube is a set of electron guns that fire a narrow beam of electrons at the screen. The image is produced, in simplified terms, by this beam racing across the screen from top to bottom in a left-to-right horizontal scanning motion. This pattern resembles your eyes' motion as you read a page of text in a book. This takes place so quickly, the viewer only sees a constant image that takes up the entire screen.

When someone watches, for example, a news show and can see reporters in the background working on computers or before a bank of TV monitors, the scanning action described above is captured. As the phosphors hit by electron beams begin to lose energy, they appear darker until instantaneously stimulated again. If the frequency of the computer or monitor isn't synchronized with the TV screen, a dark line or band will appear to slowly move up or down the screen. This explains the wavy phenomenon we see in these circumstances.

Liquid crystal displays (LCDs) and plasma screens have all but taken over the market for television and computer monitors. They use entirely different technologies than CRTs and do not create this phenomenon.

What Is a Dance Card?

Centuries ago, balls or formal dances were frequently arranged to give young ladies of means an opportunity to meet or interact with others in their social circle. Maidens were provided with a dance card when they arrived at the ball. This "card" was typically a small booklet ranging from one to three inches in size. It was often bound in leather and fitted with a charm signifying the host or theme of the dance. If the function was especially important, the dance card could be embellished with mother of pearl, gold leaf, or other fine flourishes. Inside would be a listing of all of the songs the orchestra would play during the evening—eighteen to twenty-four was typical. A cord or ribbon was attached to the dance card so that the lady could fasten it to her gown for safekeeping. A blank line would be printed by each song, allowing a prospective suitor of the young lady to request a dance and then sign his name (or she could) on the blank line next to the song if the request was granted. The last dance was usually saved for "a special someone," which led to the still-used saying, *save the last dance for me*. The dance card was intended to be a souvenir or memento of a wonderfully memorable evening.

The use of a dance card, often called *Ballspenden* from its Austrian origins, began in the eighteenth century and was quite widespread in nineteenth-century Europe, Russia, and America among affluent and influential circles. Less-affluent and less-influential folks, too, imitated this custom. Dances given by unions, manufacturing companies, schools, and civic groups were decidedly less sophisticated, with their dance cards often consisting of a simple piece of folded paper. In time, formal balls in general became less frequent and the use of dance cards fell out of favor. The dance card is a charming and fanciful artifact from yesteryear.

What Is the Diamond Sutra?

A sutra is a religious teaching or sermon of the Buddhist faith. Preached by the Buddha, sutras were memorized by disciples to pass on to subsequent generations of followers. The Diamond Sutra (AD 868) is the first known complete, printed, and dated book; the Gutenberg Bible, printed in the 1450s, was printed with moveable type and was the first book to be mass produced.

Found hidden in a sealed cave in China, the Diamond Sutra is a scroll composed of seven strips of paper printed by means of carved wooden blocks. It got its name from text within the sutra. When the disciple, Subhuti, asked the Buddha what the sutra should be called, his response was "The Diamond of Transcendent Wisdom." Its content was intended to encourage followers to cut like a diamond blade through the illusions of reality that surround mankind to reveal what is true and everlasting. The Diamond Sutra, one of Buddhism's most sacred and significant works, can be viewed at the British Library in London.

What Is the Origin of the Dollar Sign for United States Currency?

According to the U.S. Department of the Treasury, Bureau of Engraving and Printing, the most widely accepted origin of the dollar sign ($) is Mexican or Spanish. The dollar mark may be an evolved combination of a *P*, meaning "peso," "piastre," or "pieces of eight," with a superimposed *S*, presumably indicating a plural. The peso (Spanish dollar) was widely-circulated in the United States until the U.S. government established currency and coinage parameters in post-colonial times.

Our common practice of writing the dollar sign with two vertical strokes may be the result of the Spanish peso, which depicts the Pillars of Hercules at Gibraltar on its reverse (tails) side.

What Is Dry Cleaning?

To clean clothing, a solvent is needed to remove grime and stains. In everyday laundry, water serves as the solvent in conjunction with detergent. However, some fabrics are ruined by water and, for others, water is just not effective in getting the fabric clean.

Dry cleaning, in contrast, typically uses a petroleum solvent formulated in the 1930s called perchloroethylene (*perc* for short)—not water. Once the clothes are clean, the solvent is spun out or otherwise extracted for reuse and the garment is pressed and readied for its return to the customer. Perc, however, is controversial due to its possible link with cancer and other health concerns. The U.S. Occupational Safety and Health Administration (OSHA) publishes a document that guides dry-cleaning businesses in reducing employee exposure to perc. "Wet" alternatives such as using liquid carbon dioxide (CO_2) as a cleaner exist as well and are approved by the U.S. Environmental Protection Agency (EPA) as green alternatives to perc.

According to the Drycleaning & Laundry Institute International, dry cleaning has existed in varying forms since ancient times. Professional cleaners, called *fullers*, used lye, ammonia, and a certain type of absorbent clay compound called *fuller's earth* to clean clothing for their patrons. In the 1840s, an accidental spilling of a petroleum-based liquid on oil-stained fabric caused quite a stir; it was observed that when the liquid evaporated, the stains had vanished. Dry-cleaning chemicals, equipment, and techniques have dramatically improved since that time, but it is still important to be aware of the care required when purchasing a garment and to follow the manufacturer's recommendations for best results.

What Is Egg Money?

Until the mid-1900s, most eggs were produced on small farms. The farmer's wife typically supervised a number of farm activities and sold certain products raised or produced to contribute to the family income—butter and eggs among them. Farmers' wives also often raised poultry such as geese, ducks, or turkeys for sale. Jams, jellies, garden produce, and baked goods were sold when possible, as were handmade goods like bedding, clothing, and decorative items. Money earned from these sales was referred to as *egg money*. Egg money was saved for a rainy day or used to purchase needed items for the household. Interestingly, women who used these proceeds to purchase fabric to sew quilts called the end result *egg money quilts*.

What Is Meant by the *Emperor's New Clothes*?

The Emperor's New Clothes, published in 1837, is a fairy tale written by Hans Christian Andersen. It is a story about a vain emperor who is especially proud of his sartorial splendor. He hires two weavers who tell him they can make him a grand new outfit with a very special quality: only those who can *see* the outfit's magnificent fabric are wise and worthy; those who cannot see it are fools. Naturally, the emperor is quite anxious to be able to determine which of his advisors are worthy or not and, the news spreading, the subjects of the kingdom are equally excited to see which of their neighbors will be deemed wise or stupid. Of course, there are no new clothes, but the emperor feigns delight with his "new clothing." He "wears" them in a parade and all along the parade route, his subjects, afraid of appearing foolish, pretend to see and admire the outfit, too. Finally, a child cries out, "He hasn't got any clothes on!" Knowing the child is right and that he has been duped, the emperor endures the laughter of the crowd and keeps up the pretense long enough to complete the parade.

The moral of the story is multifold: (1) One's own common sense and judgment should be factored into a situation to avoid conformist behaviors where not warranted; (2) Beware of self-deceptive vanity and surface appearances; (3) Just because others say something is so, it may or may not be; (4) Beware collective ignorance; (5) Do not let the trivial (in this case, personal vanity) interfere with your pressing duties (in this case, royal duties); (6) Use caution in dealings with others; some people make a living from cheating others. If something seems too good to be true, it probably is; and (7) Be open to the thoughts or points of view of others. Sometimes wisdom, truth, and clear thinking come from surprising sources.

The emperor has no clothes or *the emperor's new clothes* as phrases are often used today in political or social contexts to indicate a truth denied by a majority due to their fear of being perceived as ridiculous, unpatriotic, or not politically correct. Keep in mind, though, that the teller of the "truth" may be biased in his or her idea of what the truth is!

Who Was Enola Gay?

The *Enola Gay* is arguably the most famous aircraft in American history. Manufactured by the Boeing Aircraft Company, this B-29 Superfortress had four 2,200 horsepower engines, a wingspan of 141 feet 3 inches, and a height of 29 feet 7 inches. Almost four thousand of these propeller-driven bombers were built for military combat in the Pacific theater during World War II. Commander of the 509th Composite Group, Colonel Paul W. Tibbets (1915–2007) hand-picked one of fifteen B-29s built to his specifications for an impending special mission. He named the aircraft *Enola Gay* after his mother, Enola Gay Tibbets, because, as he noted, she had supported his decision to become a pilot. A short time before the mission commenced, he had the name *Enola Gay* painted on the nose of his B-29.

On the morning of August 6, 1945, Tibbets piloted the *Enola Gay* with a crew of eleven men and released an atomic bomb over Hiroshima, Japan. This was the first atomic bomb used in a populated area; it is estimated that eighty thousand people were killed instantly, with an equal number wounded and many more succumbing to radiation-related complications in the months to come.

Several days later on August 9, 1945, the *Enola Gay* served as the advance weather reconnaissance plane for the *Bockscar* on the Nagasaki atomic bombing mission. These two missions played a decisive role in ending World War II, with President Truman announcing the Japanese Emperor's unconditional surrender on August 14.

The *Enola Gay*, now fully restored, is on display at the National Air and Space Museum (Steven F. Udvar–Hazy Center) in Chantilly, Virginia.

What Is a Field Holler?

Field hollers date back to a practice of pre–Civil War slaves. While working in the tobacco, cotton, and rice fields of the South, slaves would sing about their native Africa or the hardships and suffering of slavery. Essentially, these songs followed a call-and-response pattern. One worker would initiate a song. This would be followed by others (often in neighboring fields) repeating or responding by shouting, or "hollering," a verse in return, hence *field hollers*. This helped pass the time, promoted cooperation while working, and aided in easing the mental and physical anguish of slavery.

Field hollers also served communication purposes and often included special code language to evade understanding by the field supervisor. Using rhythmic patterns in music themes was also reflected in spirituals and, later, in the lyrics of blues songs of the early twentieth century.

Interestingly, the rhythmic patterns of some contemporary hip-hop and rap music are rooted in field holler–like cadences as well.

Why Is the Opening of Men's Pants Called a *Fly*?

A fly on clothing is a flap of fabric that covers an opening and conceals the means by which that opening is closed—typically a zipper, buttons, or Velcro. It is used most frequently on men's trousers, but overcoats with fabric that overlaps to conceal buttons or a zipper also have flys. Therefore, a fly is not the buttons or zipper but, more correctly, the flap of material used to hide these mechanisms of closure. This distinction has been all but lost, and the flap and fasteners are now almost universally called a *fly*.

Fly-front trousers came into being in the 1650s, but the term *fly* did not come into usage until much later. Presumably, the act of

flight (to fly) implied flapping (to flap). In 1810, the term *fly* was used to refer to the flaps (resembling wings) that covered tent openings. By 1844, the military began calling the opening in uniform pants a *fly*, and the term quickly spread into general usage.

What Is a Foot-Candle?

Foot-candle is a dated term used as a unit of measure of illumination. It is equal to the illumination or luminous intensity produced on a surface by one standard (known) candle at a distance of one foot from the light source—hence *foot-candle*. Abbreviated FC, fc, or ftc, *foot-candle* is also written *footcandle* or *foot candle*.

Foot-candle as a term came into use in the early 1900s and was adequate in describing illumination equations of the day. However, as light technology improved (and it is still evolving), the need increased for more-precise units of measurement and related terminology. *Foot-candle* as a unit of measure is considered a nonstandard measure today. *Lumens* and *lux*, among others, are more typically used in reference to contemporary lighting. However, the term *foot-candle* is still used in photography and film production as the interest in foot-candles in these fields typically involves how much light energy reaches a given object.

Why Is Gasoline Priced in Tenths of a Gallon?

The practice of pricing gasoline in tenths has existed since the 1920s or 1930s when the automobile became part of everyday life in America. There are several schools of thought about how this pricing strategy became standardized. One explanation involves the practice of levying federal and state taxes per gallon in parts of a cent. This further complicates the method of pricing each gallon of gasoline as a percentage of each barrel of crude oil, to say nothing of added refining, distribution, marketing, and retail outlet expenses.

Others say that this practice is merely a marketing ploy. The American Petroleum Institute (www.api.org) notes that gas priced this way simply looks more affordable and, because of this, doing so has become the industry standard in North America. For example, gas priced at $4.259 seems more attractive than gas priced at $4.26.

However, with prices rounded up and the smallest coin amount being one cent, the profit from pricing gasoline in tenths favors the oil companies to the tune of hundreds of thousands of dollars a year, if not more. Interestingly, in the 1980s, Iowa took action to eliminate this misleading and seemingly unfair pricing strategy. In four years, the traditional 9/10 pricing returned via legislative maneuvering with little consumer action to repeal it.

Who Was George W. Ferris?

George Washington Gale Ferris, Jr. (1859–1896), born in Illinois, was an engineer and bridge-builder. His Pittsburgh-based firm, G. W. G. Ferris & Co., tested and inspected structural steel and other metals for railways and bridges. The World's Columbian Exposition at Chicago in 1893 lamented that it had no "wow factor" planned such as the Eiffel Tower, built as the centerpiece for the Paris Exposition of 1889. Ferris proposed a thrilling amusement attraction featuring a power-operated, tension-spoked, three-dimensional steel wheel that would stand 264 feet tall. The double-rimmed wheel, 30 feet wide with a diameter of 250 feet, would carry thirty-six passenger boxes designed to carry sixty passengers in each. He won the competition and produced what is now call the *Ferris wheel*, one of the most wildly popular, profitable, and memorable attractions in World Fair history.

Bigger wheels have been built since that time, but in its day the Ferris wheel was a sensation and still bears its originator's name. For more information and a picture of the original Ferris wheel, visit: www.hydeparkhistory.org/newsletter.html.

How Did Google.com Get Its Name?

The website www.google.com is the brainchild of cofounders Larry Page and Sergey Brin who met at Stanford University as graduate students. Google became operational in 1998 in a sublet garage with a stated mission "to organize the world's information and make it universally accessible and useful" (www.google.com/corporate/index.html).

Google made *Time* magazine's Top Ten Best Cybertech list in 1999, which was quickly followed by numerous other awards and accolades. Now worth many billions of dollars, Google is the world's most trafficked search engine. In addition, Google users enjoy a variety of ancillary services including the popular functions Gmail, Google Earth, Google Scholar, Google Maps, Google Images—and many, many more.

The name *Google* comes from a play on the word *googol*, the mathematical term for the number represented by 1 followed by 100 zeros. *Googol* was reportedly coined as a term by nine-year-old Milton Sirotta when asked by his uncle, renowned American mathematician Edward Kasner, to invent a word for a really big number.

What Is a Grifter?

A grifter is a person who cheats or deceives others in some way. Often associated with taking advantage of someone for money, this term can apply to any sort of con artist, scammer, or swindler.

Typically, a grifter will form a personal or business relationship with the victim (often called the *mark*). Then, appealing to that person's weaknesses—greed, the need to be cared for, or loneliness, for example—the grifter will attempt to bribe, control, or blackmail the individual.

The term *grifter* is an Americanism coined in the early 1900s from a portmanteau combination of *graft* (swindling) and *drifter* (someone of transient residence). It was typically used for someone who ran a sideshow in a traveling circus, particularly if the person was involved in questionable gambling operations. In time, *grifter* was generalized to refer to anyone who takes advantage of someone else for monetary or personal gain. As an example, Tareq and Michaele Salahi, the couple who crashed a White House state dinner in 2009, were dubbed *grifters* by the press.

Who Were the Harvey Girls?

The Harvey Girls were women who worked for Fred Harvey (1835–1901) in his restaurant chain in southwestern America. His Harvey House Restaurant opened in Topeka, Kansas, in 1876 and led to a string of Harvey House restaurants and hotels along the Santa Fe Railway route. The company reached its pinnacle in 1917 under the management of Harvey's sons with one hundred Harvey eateries plus a number of hotels and dining cars.

Because his earlier male employees were often lawless and uncultured, Harvey advertised in the East for educated, single women between the ages of eighteen and thirty to staff his eating establishments. At that time, it was not customary for women to work unless as a teacher, nurse, or domestic. Women who worked for a living were often deemed of low social standing and questionable moral character. Nonetheless, women applied in droves due in large measure to the lure of economic stability, marital possibilities, and the excitement of testing their own mettle in new and exciting places.

Called *Harvey Girls*, never *waitresses*, these young women were under contract with strict guidelines regarding most aspects of their lives to assure good personal reputations and the good reputation of the Fred Harvey Company. Harvey Girls were well-trained for their job and held to high standards of professional service and personal conduct. They were expected to further the Harvey mission of good food, polite service, and elegant surroundings—the *Harvey way*! Because of this, the Harvey Girls are recognized for their role in helping "civilize" the West.

What Is the Hippocratic Oath?

The Hippocratic Oath is ascribed to the ancient Greek physician Hippocrates (c. 460–380 BC). However, the oath did not become well-known until years later and the author, in truth, is unknown. The Hippocratic Oath has changed dramatically over the centuries to better reflect evolving culture and medical advances. Perhaps the most surprising element related to this document is the near universally held belief that it includes the dictum "First, do no harm." However, this appears nowhere in the ancient, original version, although the principle is alluded to in a statement of the necessity "to abstain from doing harm."

The original oath speaks to personal and professional conduct, patient privacy, ethical considerations, and an indication that failing to live up to the oath will bring disgrace from a cadre of gods and goddesses.

Most contemporary medical students take some form of the Hippocratic Oath, although it departs in many ways from the ancient version. An example of a modern version was written in 1964 by

Louis Lasagna, academic dean of the School of Medicine at Tufts University. Additional information can be viewed at www.pbs .org/wgbh/nova/body/hippocratic-oath-today.html. Other oaths in use are the "Prayer of Maimoides," the "Declaration of Geneva," and the "Reinstatement of the Hippocratic Oath." The oath was not routinely required of graduating physicians for centuries. Only within the twentieth century did it become widely and consistently taken by graduating medical students.

Some physicians argue that the oath has become invalid, especially in a time of particularly thorny ethical issues related to medicine. However, others consider it to be representative of an ideal, or gold standard, as it emphasizes treating patients ethically, to the height of one's ability, and with confidentiality. Rather than a legally binding oath, it is a symbol of the care, commitment, and solemnity brought to a profession devoted to the care of fellow human beings.

In the Rhyme, Why Did Jack Jump Over the Candlestick?

Jack be nimble,
Jack be quick,
Jack jumped over the candlestick.

This nursery rhyme of Mother Goose fame has its roots in several aspects of British history. It is widely speculated that "Jack" is linked to Black Jack, an English pirate who was known for his slippery escapes from the authorities—nimble indeed.

The candle-jumping part likely came from lace-makers and the November 25 celebration of their patron saint, St. Catherine. Part of the festivities involved an amusing game that required participants to jump over a two-foot-tall lighted candle. Part sport, part fortune-telling, it was said that if one could jump over the candle

without knocking it over or extinguishing the flame, good luck was ensured for the coming year. "Candle leaping" became very popular throughout England, but due to its inherent danger, it had greatly faded in popularity by the late 1800s.

Who Is Jeff Koons?

Jeff Koons, born and raised in York, Pennsylvania, is a contemporary artist branded as a genius, charlatan, and everything in between. At the very least, he is a controversial artist and has been compared in pop status to Andy Warhol. Often dismissed as a purveyor of kitsch, Koons commands millions for his sculptures and other works of art—and gets it!

Koons, born in 1955, was educated at the Maryland Institute College of Art in Baltimore (which included an exchange year at the Art Institute of Chicago). He sold commodities to earn a living for a period of time while he continued to work on his art. In the mid-1980s, he gained attention with his Equilibrium series, followed by an extensive body of work using a range of materials including oil on canvas, polychromed aluminum and wood, mirror-finished stainless steel, vinyl, and ceramic. He exhibits internationally and is featured in many important collections, including those of the

Museum of Modern Art (New York), the Guggenheim Museum (New York), the Hirshhorn Museum (Washington, DC), and the Tate Gallery (London).

Perhaps his most widely known works are his mammoth, outdoor floral installations on permanent public display such as *Puppy* (Guggenheim Bilbao, Bilbao, Spain) and *Split-Rocker* (Papal Palace, Avignon, France). Other widely known works include *Balloon Dog*, *Rabbit*, *Hanging Heart*, and *Michael Jackson and Bubbles*. Despite the mixed reaction to his art, Koons views his work as accessible to everybody and is quoted as saying, "I'm always trying to create work that doesn't make viewers feel they're being spoken down to, so that they feel open participation."

What Is Meant by *Put Your John Hancock Here*?

John Hancock (1737–1793), born in what is now Quincy, Massachusetts, graduated from Harvard at the age of seventeen and worked as a merchant with the uncle who raised him. Upon his uncle's death, Hancock inherited the business and considerable wealth. He became increasingly disgruntled with England's impositions on citizens and businesses in the colonies—among others, the Stamp Act of 1765. He, as well as a number of other businessmen, began smuggling products and goods into the colonies to avoid what they considered unfair and burdensome taxes.

With an emphasis on outwitting and protesting British intrusions, Hancock's reputation as a patriotic hero grew, and he became a driving force for independence from England. In 1775, Hancock was elected president of the Continental Congress and, as such, was the first to sign the Declaration of Independence, adopted on July 4, 1776. It is said that he intentionally wrote his signature in the center of the signature portion of the document large enough for King George III to read without his glasses. This bold and flamboyant act became legend, and in time, *putting your John Hancock here* became synonymous with signing one's signature on a document.

Who Was Nikita Khrushchev?

Nikita Khrushchev (1894–1971) served as the first secretary of the Communist Party of the Soviet Union. Born into poverty, Khrushchev found success in politics and rose through the party's ranks. At the conclusion of World War II, he became one of Stalin's top advisors and upon Stalin's death, as a result of a brief and violent power struggle, became the head of the party in 1953. In 1958, he became premier. Khrushchev served in both positions until 1964.

Khrushchev is credited with softening the brutality and excesses of the Stalin regime by easing censorship and promoting advances in technology and agriculture. He, however, carried his own offences, notably a fervent belief that communism would conquer capitalism; responsibility for the harsh suppression of dissidents; support of the building of the Berlin Wall; and responsibility for the destruction of most churches and places of worship in the Soviet Union. Despite the so-called relaxation of Soviet conduct under Khrushchev, the Iron Curtain remained firmly in place and the Cold War continued.

Khrushchev is remembered as a volatile and flamboyant leader. He was quietly deposed by the Communist Party in 1964, a few years after the Soviet embarrassment suffered by the Cuban Missile Crisis (1962) and other missteps—not the least of which was the mortification caused by his intemperate antics at the United Nations in 1960 when he banged his shoe on the podium.

What Is Kitsch?

Kitsch is a word applied to something that is popular, mass-produced, and typically considered lowbrow and cheap—in a word, tacky! Art, decorative items, sentimental literature, or fashion may fall into this category. Naturally, what is or is not kitsch is in the eye of the beholder; what is kitsch to one person, may be a valued thing of beauty, coolness, or nostalgia to another. Pink plastic flamingos or gnome yard ornaments, for example, may be regarded as kitsch by some and as charming decorations by others. At the opposite end of the spectrum, the work of American artist Jeff Koons is widely panned as *kitsch*, yet he commands millions for his art and is widely sought after to design and create outdoor installations.

The term *kitsch* is of German origin from the mid-nineteenth century meaning "rubbish" or "cheap." The *Oxford English Dictionary* defines kitsch objects as "art or objects d'art characterized by worthless pretentiousness."

Who Was Little Lord Fauntleroy?

Little Lord Fauntleroy, authored by Frances Hodgson Burnett in 1886, has been a popular children's book for many decades, although perhaps less so in recent years. The storyline focuses on the life of a young boy, Cedric Errol, the son of a British father of aristocratic roots and an American mother. Cedric, or Ceddie, lives with his mother in New York (his father is deceased) and is a kind and loving child. His paternal grandfather, an earl in England, convinces Ceddie's mother to allow Ceddie to live in England where he will be Lord Fauntleroy and, upon the death of his grandfather, will become Earl of Dorincourt. The earl does not like America or anything American—which includes Ceddie's mother.

Desiring to foster the ways of the aristocracy in the boy, the grandfather finds that it is *he* who is transformed by Ceddie in ways of deepened humanity, kindness to the poor, and the responsibility that comes with privilege. The earl also, in time, mends his relationship with Ceddie's mother and comes to realize that it is she who has molded and shaped this remarkable child.

Upon publication, this book instantly started a little Lord Fauntleroy fashion craze, with parents from all stations in life rushing to acquire fancy velvet party suits for their sons replete with kneepants (or bloomer knickers), lace collars, and floppy bows— outfits most assuredly despised by legions of young boys on both sides of the "pond."

Although less common now, referring to a boy as a *little Lord Fauntleroy* or simply a *Fauntleroy* is synonymous with the boy being extremely polite, well-mannered, and well-dressed. The expression can be used with positive or negative connotations. Examples of usage include (1) I was so proud of Eric in his new suit—a regular little Lord Fauntleroy; and (2) John's loutish father scoffed at his son's table manners, exclaiming, "When in life do you think you will need a butter knife? I don't want to raise a Fauntleroy!"

What Is a Lobbyist?

The term *lobbyist* comes from a practice common in the English Parliament. It refers to petitioners who would await legislative members in the outer corridors, hallways, and reception rooms (hence, *lobby*) in hopes of "chatting up" lawmakers in order to sway them to their cause or point of view. Lobbying was an active practice in the fashion stated above even at the first seating of the U.S. Congress in Philadelphia in 1789. The term itself is often credited to President Ulysses S. Grant, who was often pressed by special-interest individuals and groups. This attribution, however, is unlikely as the term was in common use in the 1840s in Britain.

Lobbyist as we know it today has changed very little in meaning. It is still used to refer to the practice of individuals, groups, or organizations attempting to influence legislation. The First Amendment to the U.S. Constitution guarantees the right of the people to petition their government; however, due to the great potential of running afoul of ethical considerations, many state and federal laws have been put in place to regulate the practice of lobbying both in the United States and abroad.

Why Are London Police Officers Called *Bobbies*?

Until the early 1800s, London was patrolled by a system of watchmen and patrols to keep the citizenry safe. In 1828, the home secretary, Sir Robert Peel, introduced a bill in Parliament to establish an official, professional police force to prevent crime. Called the Metropolitan Police Service (MPS; sometimes referred to simply as the "Met"), the new police officers were called "Bobbies," or sometimes "Peelers," after their founder. Sir Peel was an unpopular man, so these nicknames were first used in derision. However, due to the success of the force, the term *bobbies* is now clearly a point of pride and a term of endearment for the most part.

The MPS, housed in New Scotland Yard, polices the Greater London area with the exception of the "square mile" of the City of London, which has its own police force. More than thirty-one thousand officers cover a territory of about 624 square miles. Bobbies wear dark-blue uniforms with white shirts and domed helmets, which may vary in accordance with duty and rank. They patrol on foot, in cars, in boats, on horseback, or by bike or scooter. Bobbies carry pepper spray, handcuffs, and a short, wooden truncheon or nightstick. Some bobbies carry firearms if the mission is dangerous.

What Is a Lotus-Eater?

The mythological lotus-eaters are described in Homer's *Odyssey*. They were people who lived on the north coast of Africa and, as would be obvious, ate lotus. Eating the lotus plant made them blissfully or dreamily forgetful, idle, and lethargic. Those of Odysseus's men who ate the lotus forgot about their friends and homeland and wished to stay among the lotus-eaters forever. Odysseus had to have his men dragged back to the ship and chained to the rowing-benches until the ship could get underway. "The Lotos-Eaters" by Alfred Lord Tennyson (1809–1892) chronicled this story, introducing it to a new, broader audience (http://charon.sfsu.edu/tennyson/LOTOS.HTML).

To say someone *eats lotus* or is a *lotus-eater* has been used for centuries to indicate forgetfulness and is also often used today in speaking of a lazy or indulgent person whose pleasure and luxury in living is a priority.

How Did the Loveseat Get Its Name?

The loveseat has its origins in the Victorian era (1837–1901). During that time, there were strict rules governing the courtship process. Physical contact between an unmarried man and woman was considered an inappropriate act of intimacy under most circumstances. Most courting occurred in the home of the woman under the watchful eye of a parent or chaperone.

Two types of loveseats were in use. The original was basically a wide chair that was designed to accommodate a woman and her voluminous dress. A second type of chair, known as a *courting chair* or *courting bench*, was built to accommodate two people, but designed in two sections in an S configuration that allowed a courting couple to sit close to one another—but not too close!

A loveseat today is typically a small sofa designed to seat two people. Naturally, if two people are seated on a loveseat at the same time, they must sit next to each other, hence the name. The Victorian S-type seat is still in existence, albeit rare.

What Is a Mausoleum?

A mausoleum (pl.: *mausolea*) is a building erected as a monument to a deceased person and features a burial chamber for the remains of the deceased. It can serve as the final resting place for one or more people and ranges from a simple, free-standing structure to something quite magnificent.

When Mausolus (377–353 BC), king of Caria in Asia Minor (now Turkey), died, his queen, Artemisia, was grief-stricken and decided to build a tribute to him in the form of the most magnificent tomb the world had ever known. Built on a hill overlooking the capital city of Halicarnassus, the resulting structure was so splendid, it is now considered one of the Seven Wonders of the Ancient World. Of note, Artemisia died two years after her husband, and she was buried with him in the unfinished tomb. Much to their credit, the craftsmen and artisans of the tomb elected to complete the structure due to its architectural significance and as a testament to their own work.

Photo by the author, photo editing by Richard S. "Chip" Russell

The mausoleum stood for seventeen centuries but was then severely damaged by a series of earthquakes. The ruins were plundered during the following centuries and by the early 1400s, only the base remained. At that point, further decimation occurred, the bodies of Mausolus and Artemisia disappeared, and important artifacts were taken for use at Bodrum Castle nearby where they remain to this very day. Other artifacts are on display at the British Museum in London. Mausolus's name is forevermore associated with this form of grand, aboveground tomb.

What Is a Mid-life Crisis?

Building on the work of noted Swiss psychiatrist Carl Jung (1875–1961), psychologist Elliott Jaques (1917–2003) coined the expression *mid-life crisis* in 1965. However, the term was not popularized until the next decade with Gail Sheehy's best-selling book *Passages: Predictable Crises of Adult Life*. *Mid-life crisis* is a term generally applied to certain emotional transitions that may occur between the ages of forty and sixty. For most, this experience is a normal part of life and any distress experienced is short-lived. However, some individuals sink into a profound depression and require professional help.

Typical mid-life crisis emotions include unhappiness with one's life, lifestyle, or accomplishments; disenchantment with one's job; dissatisfaction with or bitterness toward one's spouse or other family members; and feeling the need for new challenges, adventures, or experiences. Some individuals feel the need to prove something to themselves or others. These and other feelings may inexplicably occur even if the individual is otherwise satisfied and may be complicated by the belief that their life is quickly passing by, that youth is over with no real prospect of meaningful change in the future, and that old age is impending. The desire for major change may be triggered or intensified by other key life events such as children leaving home, the death of a parent, and arriving at one of the big "0" birthdays.

Often stereotyped or made the butt of jokes, a mid-life crisis may actually serve as a motivator for taking stock and making positive, major life changes such as returning to school, engaging in a spiritual awakening, or committing to volunteer work for the common good.

What Is a Muse?

In Greek mythology, Zeus, king of all the gods, and Mnemosyne, goddess of memory, had nine daughters known as the *Muses*. The

Muses represented different arts and sciences, ruled over them, and provided inspiration for artists and scholars in their given area of importance. As examples, Calliope was muse of epic song; Terpsichore, muse of dance; and Urania, muse of astronomy. Men whom the daughters loved had their troubles and worries disappear; these men became revered by all who knew them. From *muse*, we get the words *music*, *museum*, and *mosaic*.

Since ancient times, men and women of the arts have been inspired, encouraged, and sustained by their own muses. A muse is in the eye of the artist and most often is a loved one considered indispensible to the artist's creativity and productivity; they often become a featured subject or co-creator of a work. Muses can be public, private, or spiritual. Picasso had "serial muses." His work documents his many love interests throughout a large portion of his career.

What Is a Nemesis?

In Greek mythology, Nemesis was the goddess of indignation with and retribution for wicked acts and undeserved good fortune. Her name is a derivative of the Greek word for "dispenser of dues." She kept balance in human affairs regarding happiness and unhappiness, success (or lack thereof) in love, material blessings, and the like. If the balance became askew, particularly if someone was having too great of a life in some regard or if a wrong was committed without penalty, Nemesis would avenge this by inflicting loss, suffering, or vengeance. This belief purportedly helped keep people in check so that they would self-regulate themselves in order to prevent action by Nemesis.

Nemesis's name is now used (uncapitalized) to describe a person or thing that is a source of harm or damage and to indicate a formidable, and typically victorious, opponent. Examples of its usage include (1) Self-doubt is Barbara's nemesis; it bests her efforts every time; (2) The Praxis I tests were Tony's nemesis. He took them multiple times, but just could not pass them; and (3) After losing five consecutive seasons to Farmingham's football team, we hoped at long last we would beat our nemesis this year.

What Is Occam's Razor?

Occam's (ah-kums) razor, sometimes *Ockham's razor*, is a philosophical and scientific principle of simplicity. William of Occam (Ockham), an early-fourteenth-century Franciscan friar and logician, tired of the fuzzy logic and loquacious tendencies of his contemporaries and asserted succinctly, "Entities should not be multiplied unnecessarily." His philosophy was to shave away all unnecessary or extraneous material or thoughts.

Occam also advanced the notion of empiricism, that is, using evidence to formulate ideas and knowledge. He believed that theories help explain and predict the natural world and that theories can more easily be arrived upon by making fewer assumptions about the topic contemplated. He was considered quite radical in his time, advocating for freedom of speech and separation of church and state, to name a few, but he was a courageous, clear-thinking man as well. It was Sir William Hamilton in 1852 who, based on Occam's thinking, coined the term *Occam's razor* as it is used today.

Occam's razor is also known as the "principle of parsimony," which, in essence, means the simplest explanation is often the most likely to be correct. Today, the concept of Occam's razor is used in scientific, medical, religious, and political discussions. It is also used in everyday speech, for example, "Using Occam's razor, I concluded that over two hundred townspeople attended the dreary annual board meeting not because they were part of a secret conspiracy to take over the meeting, but because free coffee and doughnuts were available."

What Is an Old Wives' Tale?

Simply put, an old wives' tale is a traditional belief, often rooted in superstition. Despite its negative connotation toward older women, the term *old wives' tale* endures and is commonly used today. Dating to at least the times of ancient Greece, a similar phrase was used in the English language as early as the late 1300s.

Old wives' tales are part of our oral tradition in which stories are passed down from generation to generation. They often involve the curative powers of common objects, tokens of good or bad luck, and the predictive powers of certain phenomena. Most of them are false or just plain nonsense. Examples include (1) Feed a cold, starve a fever; (2) Toads cause warts; (3) A cat on a ship brings good luck; and (4) A ring suspended by a string over the belly of an expectant mother will indicate the gender of the child, depending on the movement of the ring.

What Materials Are Used to Make Olympic Medals?

The International Olympic Committee (IOC) stipulates that each Olympic medal be at least three millimeters thick and sixty millimeters in diameter. Both the gold and silver medals are required to contain 92.5 percent silver, with the gold medal then plated with no fewer than six grams of 24-karat gold. Bronze medals are composed of copper, zinc, tin, and a tiny amount of silver. The last Olympic medals made of solid gold were awarded at the 1912 Stockholm Olympics.

The practice of awarding Olympic medals was initiated at the 1896 Athens Games with the revival of the modern Olympics. In ancient Greece, medals were not awarded: the first-place winner of each contest was given an olive-branch headpiece; other contestants received nothing.

What Does *P.A.* after an Attorney's Name Mean?

Incorporating an enterprise affords businesspersons certain opportunities to raise capital, take advantage of tax benefits, and limit personal liability. Inclusion of *Incorporated*, *Company*, or *Corporation* in the name of a company typically signifies the company's status as an incorporated business. Every state sets its own rules of incorporation and regulates types of corporate options for regular and professional businesses.

Members of certain professions who provide professional services may also benefit from incorporating for the same reasons noted above even though they typically differ in purpose and size from traditional businesses: lawyers, physicians, architects, engineers, and accountants, for example. As such, particular rules of incorporation apply to them, and their options may include forming a professional association (P.A.), a professional company (P.C.), or a limited liability corporation (L.L.C., P.L., or L.P.). These, as noted, will vary in accordance with state statutes. They are often written *PA, PC, LLC, PL*, and *LP*.

In Measurement, What Is a Peck?

In the United States' customary system, a peck is a unit of dry or liquid measure. It corresponds to 537.6 cubic inches (dry) or

9.31 quarts (liquid). Contemporary usage of this unit of measure is limited and is almost always reserved for dry commodities such as grain, fruit, and berries. At farm markets, apples may be sold in peck or half-peck bags or baskets. Four pecks equal one bushel.

The origin of the term *peck* is somewhat obscure, but it is likely the term is taken from the Latin *picotinus*, a measure of grain, and *picotus*, a liquid measure. Perhaps the best-known usage of *peck* is in the Mother Goose verse:

> *Peter Piper picked a peck of pickled peppers;*
> *A peck of pickled peppers, Peter Piper picked;*
> *If Peter Piper picked a peck of pickled peppers,*
> *Where's the peck of pickled peppers Peter Piper picked?*

What Is a Pince-Nez?

A pince-nez (pans-nay) is a type of eyewear that clips to the bridge of the nose. Usually rimless, they have no sidepieces (the parts of traditional eyeglasses that fit on either side of one's face and end behind the ears), and no handle (like opera glasses). Although available in some form since the fifteenth century, the pince-nez reached its peak in popularity in the nineteenth century and into the early twentieth. Sometimes called *nose-spectacles* or *Oxford glasses*, the pince-nez is fitted to the nose by way of a flexible, adjustable bridge or by spring tension.

From the French *pincer* (to pinch) and *nez* (nose), a pince-nez is often tethered to the wearer for safety and convenience, especially if used as reading glasses. Worn by men (as did President Roosevelt—see p. 169) and women alike, the pince-nez is often considered today as antiquarian. However, they are still available at many eyewear providers.

Courtesy of the Library of Congress, LC-USZ62-13026

Why Are British Hunting Coats Called *Pinks*?

A *pink* is the scarlet coat traditionally worn by fox hunters, or the cloth used to make such attire. There are several theories as to how this garment got its name. The most popular involves eighteenth-century London tailor Thomas Pink (or possibly Pinke, or Pinque), a popular maker of such coats. Due to the quality of his work, wearing a Pink garment became synonymous with wealth and aristocratic good taste. In time, the name was generalized to apply to all scarlet riding coats regardless of maker.

Some speculate, instead, that *pinks* is taken from the idiom *in the pink*, meaning "being perfect" or "being the best." Others say that *in the pink* refers to actually wearing a pink garment; however, this is unlikely as this idiom dates back to at least the 1500s. Regardless of the origin of the term *pinks*, the color red was probably originally chosen as a safety color—much like hunters today wearing orange when hunting.

How Did Polka Dots Get Their Name?

Polka dancing was enormously popular in mid-nineteenth-century America and Europe. Savvy merchants and marketers named a number of products polka-this and polka-that. Toward the end of the century, a new fabric was introduced featuring uniformly sized and spaced dots and, true-to-form for the time, this pattern was called *polka dots*—a clear and successful attempt to cash in on the polka-dancing craze. It is not certain if wearing dotted garb was specifically associated with dancing the polka, but polka dot men's and women's clothing alike was widely available for purchase as was polka dot fabric for home seamstresses.

Polka dot fabric remains fashionable today as does polka dancing, although neither are as universally popular as in yesteryear.

What Is a Ponzi Scheme?

According to the U.S. Securities and Exchange Commission, a Ponzi scheme is a type of illegal pyramid operation where a con artist secures money from investors using the lure of quick and easy money. The earliest investors often receive good (even impressive) returns, but this money comes from the money paid by more-recent investors and not from gains from the purported investments. In time, the scam collapses as fewer and fewer investors realize any profit. The newest investors are often tantalized by what they see that earlier investors made, which encourages them to undertake bigger risks, and almost always eventually lose the money they invest. Ponzi schemes are often referred to as *rob Peter to pay Paul* operations.

Ponzi schemes are named after Charles Ponzi (1882–1949), a handsome and charming Italian immigrant who, between 1920 and 1921, bilked $10 million from those investing in his postal currency scheme; this was a bogus operation based on differences between domestic and foreign currencies and mailing coupons. Eventually, he served prison time for his actions and was later deported to Italy. His last years were spent in South America where he died in a charity hospital in Rio de Janeiro. His name is now forever linked to financial fraud.

In the news in 2009 we saw the conviction of Bernard L. Madoff for securities fraud in a classic Ponzi scheme where he reported inflated returns on investments and paid his investors with the money invested by newer investors. It is estimated that upward of $50 billion was involved in this swindle involving people from all walks of life, many of them losing their entire life savings.

What Are the Duties of the President of the United States?

The functions, powers, and responsibilities of the president are outlined in Article II of the Constitution of the United States. As head of the executive branch, the president has a major role in law-making as he approves or vetoes bills set before him by Congress. A veto can be overridden by a two-thirds Congressional majority. The president can propose a bill, but cannot write one. He is also charged with the responsibility of ensuring that laws are faithfully executed, typically though cabinet-level departments and other federal agencies.

Among his duties, the president acts as head of state and commander-in-chief of the armed forces. He names appointees to cabinet posts; makes treaties; appoints ambassadors; names Supreme Court judges and other federal judges; oversees foreign policy; and fills vacancies that may occur during a Senate recess. Many of these functions require Senate majority approval. The president may also grant reprieves and pardons for offences against the United States (except in cases of impeachment); deliver the State of the Union address; receive foreign ambassadors or other public ministers; and commission all officers of the United States.

The president at this writing makes an annual salary of $400,000 plus a $50,000 non-taxable expense allowance to assist in defraying expenses relating to or resulting from the discharge of official duties. To read Article II of the U.S. Constitution, visit http://caselaw .lp.findlaw.com/data/constitution/article02.

What Is a Presidential Executive Order?

An executive order (EO) is a declaration issued by the president (or governor at the state level) that has the force of law. EOs are intended to direct administrative agencies in performing functions sanctioned by law or congressional action, although they sometimes can seem to be contradictory.

Legally binding, EOs are typically orders based on statutory authority and require no action by Congress. Presidential authorization to issue EOs is found in Article II, Sections 1 and 3 of the Constitution. Executive orders often fall into certain broad categories that include ceremonial or symbolic proclamations, national security directives, and treaty negotiations.

Sometimes controversial, EOs can be legislatively or judicially challenged within established parameters. Executive orders are numbered and published in the *Federal Register* and under Title 3 of the *Code of Federal Regulations* since 1936. They can be viewed at www.whitehouse.gov/briefing-room/presidential-actions.

What Is a Rhinestone?

A rhinestone is a clear or colored artificial gem made of glass, crystal, acrylic, gem quartz, or paste. It got its name because the original rhinestones were pieces or pebbles of rock crystal sifted from the Rhine along Austria's western boundary. Prized for centuries because of their resemblance to diamonds, these stones were hand cut and finished by hand, and were quite pricey. In 1892, Daniel Swarovski patented a machine to cut facets in glass jewelry stones with precision and speed and with a quality and brilliance that far surpassed that of the hand-cut stones. Over the years, improvements in technology have been made. In addition, improvements have been enacted regarding the quality of the materials used, the cut, and the backing of each bit of glass, for which gold, silver, tin, or tinted foil is used to achieve the desired effect.

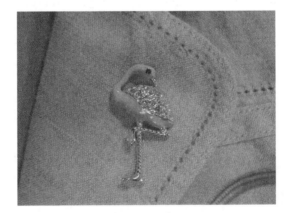

Rhinestones are tremendously popular for the glitz and glamour they add to show, dance, and skating costumes as well as to wedding apparel and costume jewelry. Rhinestones are manufactured primarily in Austria, although Czech and Korean rhinestones are readily available. Swarovski and Company rhinestones are made of fine lead crystal with eight or fourteen facets and are widely considered to be of the highest quality. Rhinestones, however, require special care. Rhinestone jewelry must be stored separately to avoid scratching the stones. It must not be allowed contact with water as this may promote tarnish of the backing metal or softening of the glue used to affix the stones.

Are the Things Presented in Ripley's Believe It or Not! True?

LeRoy "Robert" Ripley (1890–1949) was quite a celebrity in the first half of the twentieth century. A self-taught artist and accomplished athlete, Ripley worked for the *New York Globe* as a sports cartoonist. On a slow day, he decided to illustrate and present several unusual sports events. An instant success, the feature was named "Champs and Chumps," but soon thereafter Ripley renamed it "Believe It or Not."

Ripley, an intrepid daredevil and explorer, traveled extensively in over two hundred countries, seeking facts about human oddities. He also collected artifacts to support his claims, which eventually formed the basis for his extensive, bizarre, and interesting collections. Today, Ripley Entertainment, a Canadian-based corporation, boasts a Ripley cartoon circulation in over two hundred newspapers worldwide and sixty-five attractions in twelve countries, including numerous museums (called *odditoriums* and based in large measure on display items collected by Ripley himself). There are also Ripley-associated aquariums, wax museums, and miniature golf attractions.

The general public is encouraged to submit weird or strange facts to www.ripleys.com for inclusion in the newspaper cartoon feature. Documentation authenticating truthfulness and accuracy is required. There have been challenges to Ripley claims over the years; in fact, Robert Ripley laughed at being called a liar, stating that "there's nothing stranger than the truth." Defying logic and imagination, even today, we are often left wondering: *Do we believe it or not?*

What Does the Symbol ℞ Mean?

The symbol ℞ is used to signify a prescription medication. It is often seen as *Rx* because some word processors do not feature the ℞ symbol. Taken from Latin, the *R* is short for *recipere*, meaning "to take." The lowercase *x* is not an *x* at all, but a diagonal line drawn through the tail of the *R*. It is thought to represent the mythological Roman deity Jupiter. Jupiter, king of the gods, was the father of Apollo, the god of healing. The reference to Jupiter is believed to represent a petition seeking Jupiter's blessings on the drug to assure the recovery of the patient.

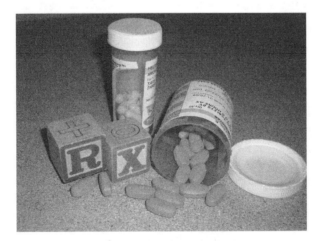

Pharmacies and apothecaries have displayed this symbol for centuries as a form of communication to patients of their ability to correctly interpret and fill the orders of physicians.

What Is Meant by *Performance Sandbagging*?

Sandbagging is a term that has come to mean several things. Perhaps the most common usage is in reference to deliberately under-performing at something or downplaying one's skills in preliminary trials in order to hide one's true potential; this is done to provide a tactical advantage by keeping one's competitors in the dark. We often see the term *sandbagging* used in this way in gambling, tennis, golf, and other sports.

Sandbagging is used in business when employees understate their performance objectives or goals so that their actual performance gives the appearance of far exceeding expectations. Sandbagging can also be used by a winning contender to limit the margin of victory to avoid humiliating an opponent. Another use of the term *sandbagging* simply refers to a person's being generally unhurried or lazy at accomplishing something.

The 1887 origin of this term as a verb rests not in the act of filling bags with sand for purposes of flood control but in acts of ambush. In this sense, hooligans would fill socks or small bags with sand to hurl or swing at their victims in order to deliver a painful blow, but leave no marks.

Who Coined the Phrase *Say Goodnight, Gracie*?

George Burns (1896–1996) was one of the most celebrated and beloved comedians of the twentieth century. An Academy Award–winning actor, author, singer, and dancer, his career spanned Vaudeville, film shorts, feature films, radio, television and the Las Vegas stage. Burns produced TV shows in the 1960s, including the popular *Mr. Ed*. He was an energetic entertainer who continually reinvented himself and actively worked in show business until just a short time before his death at the age of one hundred.

Part of George Burns's comedic success is credited to his chance meeting with Grace Ethel Cecile Rosalie Allen (1902–1964).* Known as Gracie Allen, she was first Burns's comedy partner, but soon became his wife as well. Allen, a bright and articulate woman, played a ditsy character known for her "illogical logic" paired with Burns's straight-man persona. This dynamic and endearing pair starred in the *Burns and Allen Show*, which was a top radio show for almost twenty years. Around 1950, Burns wanted to see if their show could successfully transition to a new entertainment medium—television. This proved to be a wise move, and the *George Burns and Gracie Allen Show* ran until 1958 when Gracie Allen retired.

To close the television show, Burns and Allen would come forward to address the live studio audience. Allen would characteristically prattle on, with Burns finally stating, "Say goodnight, Gracie," to which she would say "Goodnight," and both would exit the stage. In time, the phrase *Say goodnight, Gracie* became a euphemism for *Stop talking* or *Let's conclude*.

*The year 1902 is the date given on Ms. Allen's crypt. George Burns claimed to not know her year of birth, and her birth record was destroyed in the devastating San Francisco earthquake of 1906. Sources vary on her year of birth, placing it between 1895 and 1906.

What Is the Origin of *Say It Ain't So, Joe*?

During the 1919 World Series, the Chicago White Sox were alleged to have lost to the Cincinnati Reds on purpose. Arguably the most notorious disgrace in baseball history, this became known as the *Black Sox Scandal* because it was such a dark day for the sport of baseball. Eight players were charged with, but cleared of, criminal charges; however, all eight received a permanent ban from professional baseball by Kenesaw Mountain Landis, U.S. federal judge and first commissioner of professional baseball.

One of those players banned was baseball great "Shoeless" Joe Jackson (Joseph Jefferson Jackson, 1887–1951). The nickname *Shoeless* was acquired early in Jackson's professional career. A pair of new shoes rubbed blisters on his feet and his feet hurt so badly he couldn't wear shoes, so Jackson played in his socks. Jackson's being without shoes only occurred once, but the moniker *shoeless* stuck.

It was reported in the *Chicago Daily News* on September 29, 1920, that as "Shoeless" Joe Jackson left the grand jury room, a little boy tugged on his pants and, looking up at him, pleaded with Jackson by saying, "Say it ain't so, Joe, say it ain't so." In a later interview, "Shoeless" Joe denied that this exchange had ever occurred—but this fabled story lived on and still represents a sense of disappointment in someone admired.

Shoeless Joe's Sports Cafe in Fort Myers, FL

Many sources concur that Jackson did not take part in the fix as he batted, fielded, and ran bases admirably during all the suspected games. It is, however, believed that he may have had knowledge of the fix prior to the series. A permanent ban prohibits a player from ever being inducted into the National Baseball Hall of Fame in Cooperstown, New York. Therefore, a number of groups over the years have continued to work to exonerate Jackson. His legend lives on and his name graces a number of commercial enterprises, including independent and franchise restaurants.

What Is Meant by *Seeding* in Sports?

Seeding in athletics means to arrange individual players or teams according to their athletic ability, performance, or other criteria depending on the sport. It is a ranking of players or teams and a predictor of success based on past performance. *Seed* in this sense is an Americanism dating at least to 1898 in reference to American lawn tennis. The usage meant to sort players so that players in each class of play were separated by skill or other criteria—a metaphor likening players or teams to the scattering of seeds in a garden a certain distance apart for maximum results in growth.

The ultimate goal was (and is) to not have the strongest, most proficient players or teams square off until the later stages of the tournament. This is essentially the idea today when we speak of *top seeds* or the assignment of a number—first seed, second seed, and so on. This system, determined by an often complicated set of criteria that varies from sport to sport, gives lower-seeded players or teams a chance to compete with similarly skilled competitors. This tends to add excitement to the entire tournament as audiences love to see so-called underdogs advance in play—*Cinderella stories*, they are often called. In addition, staging a tournament using these strategic brackets builds anticipation as fans clamor to see the top-seeded players compete.

Why Did Ladies Ride Sidesaddle in Yesteryear?

Sidesaddle horse riding, or riding *aside* as it is often called, was the preferred and expected mode of riding a horse for ladies for many centuries. Sidesaddle riding requires a special saddle designed for a rider who has both legs on one side of the horse. Amazingly, a properly trained rider and horse can hunt, jump, and engage in dressage.

At one time, riding like men, called riding *astride* or *cross-saddle*, was considered improper and immodest for women of royal lineage and other women of means. Depictions of women riding aside are seen on ancient Grecian urns, and the tradition continued in large measure until the mid-1900s, though exceptions existed, such as women riding *pillion* (astride behind men or astride with a specially designed split-skirt. However, by the eighteenth century, notables like Marie Antoinette of France (1755–1793) and Catherine the Great of Russia (1729–1796) were known to have donned men's breeches to ride cross-saddle as they saw fit.

The earliest sidesaddles were little more than a padded board. By the eleventh century, women rode aside in saddles resembling armchairs with a foot board (planchette). In time, certain design modifications were made for security and comfort with added pommels, horns, balance straps, and stirrups—much to the relief of women and horses alike.

The art of sidesaddle riding was in full force in 1920s Britain where the emphasis was on the elegance and style of the sport. World War II, however, saw a dramatic decline in sidesaddle riding. Due to shortages of material for tack and riding garb, not to mention the personnel needed to train horses and riders, the traditional riding finery worn by ladies was packed away. After the war, when people began taking up their pre-war pastimes, women almost exclusively began to wear a trouser-type riding habit and to ride cross-saddle like men.

In recent years, there has been a resurgence of interest in sidesaddle riding, primarily for show and competition. Information may be found at www.sidesaddleassociation.co.uk or www.americanside saddleassociation.org.

What Is a Silhouette?

A silhouette is the filled outline of an image set against a contrasting color, often black on white paper, and may be painted, cut from paper, or photographed. The name *silhouette* is taken directly from the name of Étienne de Silhouette, French finance minister for Louis XV. Silhouette was widely known and mocked for his parsimonious ways; the term *à la Silhouette* became synonymous for *on the cheap*. That, coupled with Silhouette's hobby of cutting paper shadow-portraits, earned silhouette portraiture its name.

Silhouettes were especially popular from 1750 to 1850 in Europe and America; they were affordable because they could be made by drawing the outline cast by candlelight. Well-known American silhouettists of the day were M. S. Doyle, Henry Williams, and William Banche. The advent of the daguerreotype, then photography as we know it today, dramatically and negatively impacted the popularity of silhouettes.

Who Was Sisyphus?

In Greek mythology, Sisyphus (sis-ih-fus) was King of Corinth. However, he committed a variety of unlawful and dishonest acts, including violent attacks on travelers and visitors in his land. Hades, god of the underworld, personally came to claim Sisyphus for the kingdom of the dead. Ever resourceful—a crafty man, indeed—Sisyphus tricked Hades and cheated death, which he did once again later with Persephone, queen of the dead. He lived on for a number of years and died at a ripe old age.

Homer, in the *Odyssey*, relates that in penance for a continuing lifetime of misdeeds and crimes against the gods, Sisyphus in the after-life was ordered to roll a "monstrous stone" up a steep hill to the summit. However, just before Sisyphus could reach the top, weight and gravity would cause the boulder to roll back down and Sisyphus would have to repeat his arduous task again, and again, and again throughout eternity. The gods considered this futile, hopeless, and monotonous task just deserts for Sisyphus's wickedness, deception, and trickery in life.

In keeping with this legend, we now invoke Sisyphus's name by describing seemingly dreary and pointless tasks or challenges as *Sisyphean*.

What Is a Sporran?

Sporran (spore-un or spar-un) is a Gaelic word for "pouch" or "purse." A sporran is worn at the front of a kilt just below the waistline on a chain or belt as part of the traditional garb of Scottish Highlanders. The earliest sporrans were leather bags made of animal skin, often deer or badger. As kilts have no pockets, the sporran's original purpose was to carry a day's supplies, rations, or other items. In time, however, it evolved from a practical, everyday pouch to more flamboyant versions for formal or dress occasions. Dress sporrans can be decorated with fur, silver ornamentation, jewels, emblems, or the long, horsehair tassels featured by familiar parade sporrans. Day or casual sporrans, however, are still often simple leather pouches adorned only with small Celtic knots or tassels.

Sporrans today are most often seen at formal Scottish events such as weddings, funerals, and other special or ceremonial occasions such as the Highland Games held annually in Ligonier, PA.

How Did the Stanley Cup Get Its Name?

The Stanley Cup, oldest trophy in professional athletics, is named after its originator Sir Frederick Arthur Stanley, the Earl of Preston and governor general of Canada. In 1892 at a dinner of the Ottawa Amateur Athletic Association, a message from Lord Stanley was read stating in part:

> I have for some time been thinking that it would be a good thing if there were a challenge cup which should be held from year to year by the champion hockey team in the Dominion [of Canada].

Lord Stanley provided a silver cup and appointed two trustees as its guardian with the express conditions that the trophy be passed to the winning team each year and that it be delivered in good condition. The winning team's name would be engraved on a silver ring attached to the cup. In the event of any dispute, the matter would be decided by the trustees.

The Stanley Cup was first awarded to the Montreal Amateur Athletic Association in 1893. In 1910, the National Hockey Association took custody of the cup, and since 1926 only National Hockey League teams have been eligible to compete for the trophy. The current custom is to have every winning team member's name engraved on the cup. Naturally, doing so would quickly create an unwieldy trophy, so engraved bands on the trophy are "retired" at regular intervals and displayed along with the original Stanley Cup at the MCI Great Hall in Toronto, Ontario.

Currently, the cup is composed of a bowl supported by three tiered bands, a collar, and a base of five uniform bands of the most recent winners' names. It measures 35.25 inches tall and weighs 34.5 pounds. Each member of the winning team is permitted to possess the cup for twenty-four hours. Consequently, the cup is well traveled and has made appearances at the White House, the Kremlin, and on various television shows; it has even been used as a baptismal font.

On the Road, What Is Tailgating?

Tailgating is a practice engaged in by some drivers when they follow another vehicle too closely. Not only is this aggressive form of driving impolite, it is also dangerous and illegal. Drivers who tailgate put themselves in a position where they cannot react effectively if an emergency arises. This puts the tailgater in danger and others as well.

Tailgating is a major cause of automobile accidents. To avoid *being* a tailgater, follow the four-second rule. Note when the rear bumper of the vehicle in front of you passes a certain point, then count the seconds until you reach the same point. If the time elapsed is less than four seconds, you are following the vehicle too closely.

Road and weather conditions may necessitate leaving an even greater space cushion between vehicles. If you find that you have a tailgater behind you on a two-lane road, wait until the road ahead is free of oncoming traffic, then flash your brake lights and (slowly) reduce your speed to encourage the tailgater to pass you.

What Is a Tinker?

A tinker was a person who traveled from town to town for the purpose of mending pots, pans, or other metal household utensils. The term *tinker* is most likely taken from the Middle English *tinnkere* or the Gaelic *tinceard* (tin worker or tinsmith), but some people suggest that the term came from the tinkling sound made when metal clicks together or when a hammer strikes metal.

Tinsmithing was (and is) an honorable profession requiring a lengthy apprenticeship and journeyman training. Some tinkers once took to the road in order to make enough money to open their own tinsmith shops. Others were hired by established tinsmiths to repair or sell wares on routes far from the shop itself. Keep in mind, centuries ago cookware was expensive and difficult to replace.

Despite the fact that tinkers served a needed and valuable purpose, the term *tinker* became a disparaging expression meaning "a beggar, thief, rogue, or person of low status." *Tinker* is still used negatively today in some locales to disparage certain itinerate individuals.

Tinker in contemporary usage signifies an act of unskillful or experimental work to fix or improve something. Examples of usage include (1) Paul knew he needed to take his car to a mechanic, but allowed his son to tinker with the engine first; (2) Sara was dissatisfied with her essay and continued to tinker with it to the point of total ruination; and (3) Robert knew little about plumbing, but was determined to tinker with his faucet until he stopped the leak.

Why Is a Pine Branch Placed at the Peak of a New Barn?

The practice of placing a pine bough or small tree at the apex of a building under construction dates to at least the Middle Ages and is taken from an ancient pagan ritual designed to honor, appease, or secure the blessings of the forest gods for using trees in the construction. Because people were so dependent on the products of the forest, many forms of reverence toward trees came into being. In time, the practice came to symbolize the hope for a long life and fertility of the land and household of the owner.

This practice is called *Richt Fest*, which means "topping out celebration," or more commonly, simply *topping out*, and is widely practiced today for all sorts of structures. Topping out came to America via European immigrants and was commonly used for barn raisings, housewarmings, and other construction projects. Today, it is not uncommon to conduct topping out ceremonies for skyscrapers, bridges, ships, or other forms of commercial or residential construction. This may take the form of attaching a small evergreen tree or bough, a flag, a steel beam painted white (sometimes signed by workers and dignitaries), or other celebratory items to the peak of a structure to signify the completion of the structure's skeleton or frame.

Topping out is often accompanied by a festive social gathering of friends or of those who have invested in the project to bring good luck and success to the structure.

Who Was Vince Lombardi?

Vincent Thomas Lombardi (1913–1970) is remembered for his legendary success as a football coach, his dedication to the sport, and his motivational style. He is credited with revitalizing the downtrodden Green Bay Packers and taking them to victory in Super Bowls I and II. Originally named the World Championship Game Trophy, this award was renamed the Vince Lombardi Trophy in 1970 prior to Super Bowl V (1971) to honor Lombardi's greatness. Lombardi was voted Coach of the Century in 2000 by ESPN.

The Vince Lombardi Trophy is presented to the Super Bowl's winning team. Until 1996, the presentation was a locker-room tradition. Since Super Bowl XXX, however, it is now an event held on the field for all to see. The winning team maintains permanent possession of its Vince Lombardi Trophy, necessitating the crafting of a new one every year. The trophy itself stands twenty-two inches tall, and is made by Tiffany and Company of sterling silver. Weighing 6.7 pounds, it portrays a regulation-size football mounted in the kicking position on a stand that resembles a concave-sided pyramid. Engraved with *Vince Lombardi Trophy*, *Super Bowl* [number], and the NFL shield, the trophy is returned to Tiffany and Company after the field ceremony so that the name of the winning team can be engraved.

What Is Voodoo?

Voodoo is a religion originating in West Africa; its name is taken from the word *vodun*, meaning "spirit." Those practicing Voodoo believe that all things on earth are interconnected, with nothing occurring by chance. Communication with a supreme deity takes place through specific spirits called *Loa*. Loa are believed to exist within many elements such as the earth, wind, certain trees, and snakes; they are responsible for the events in everyday life. A typical Voodoo service may include praying, vocalizing in secret languages, spirit-possessed dancing, casting of spells, conducting various rituals, and, typically, engaging in animal sacrifices. Trances and magical practices are also associated with Voodoo, with spirit possession and veneration of ancestors being central to Voodoo's practice.

Voodoo was brought to the New World in the 1700s and 1800s through the slave trade. Appalled at this expression of worship, the Catholic Church sought to convert Voodoo practitioners to

Christianity. Because these slaves could not openly practice Voodoo, many infused Voodoo with certain elements from Catholicism to help mask their continued practice of Voodoo—a process known as *syncretization*.

Voodoo is viewed by many as an alarming, mysterious, and sinister practice. Some of this perception has been fueled by fictional depictions and the frightening aspect of some of the rituals. Today, Voodoo is practiced in varying forms primarily in certain African nations, Haiti, Trinidad, Jamaica, Cuba, Brazil, and Louisiana, with an estimated 50 million followers.

Why Are Wedding Rings Worn on the Left Hand?

Wearing a wedding ring on the left hand, fourth finger (some consider the ring finger the third finger, not counting the thumb) is common practice in the United States, United Kingdom, Brazil, and other countries. In the days before medical science understood the circulatory system, the Romans and Egyptians believed that a blood vessel ran directly from what we refer to as the ring finger to the heart. It was given the Latin name *vena amori* (vein of love).

A further association involved the left hand being closer to the heart. Placing a wedding ring on the ring finger of the left hand

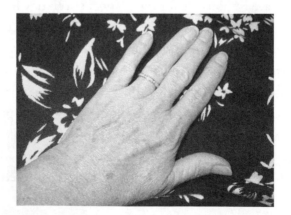

became a part of nuptial etiquette by the 1500s with the groom, as part of the ceremony, partially placing the ring on the bride's thumb, index finger, and middle finger stating for each respectively, "The Father, Son, and Holy Ghost." The ring was then placed on the bride's fourth, or ring, finger.

However, there have been times in history when the wedding ring was placed on the fourth finger of the right hand as the right hand was associated with being more righteous. Many countries today such as Norway, Germany, and Russia use the ring finger on the right hand for wedding bands.

What Are Yellow Dog and Blue Dog Democrats?

A yellow dog Democrat is simply a particular kind of voter. The term *yellow dog Democrat* is used to describe a Democratic voter, typically from the South, who is fiercely loyal to voting the party line. It comes from a 1928 election when Democrats nominated Al Smith (D-NY) as their national candidate. Disgusted, Senator Tom Heflin (D-AL) not only declined to support the Democratic candidate, he actively supported the Republican candidate, Herbert Hoover, instead; this was a situation considered nothing short of profane in the South at that time. Part of Smith's failed campaign, particularly in Alabama, included the popular slogan "I'd vote for a yellow dog if he ran on the Democratic ticket." The term *yellow dog* survived the election and is still used today as praise for a loyal Democrat.

Blue Dog Democrats, on the other hand, are Democrats in the U.S. House of Representatives who self-identify as being fiscally conservative and aligned with American mainstream values. Often characterized as being less-partisan, they are an actual voting coalition in Congress composed of more than fifty members hailing from all over the United States. According to the Blue Dog Coalition website, the Blue Dogs were so named by a comment made by former Rep. Pete Geren (D-TX), who is credited with stating that the more-liberal members of his party had "choked blue" the more-moderate members in the years preceding the 1994 election. *Blue* was then substituted for *yellow* in *yellow dog Democrat*, presumably as a play on the term. More information about the Blue Dog Coalition can be found at http://ross.house.gov/BlueDog/.

Why Are Judges Called *Your Honor*?

In the United States, *Your Honor* is considered the proper way to address a judge, justice, or magistrate in the courtroom, although it is also acceptable to say *Judge* [last name]. Mayors and other dignitaries may be addressed as *Your Honor* as well. Doing so affords these persons the level of respect that accompanies the office. In referring to judges in the third person, it is common to use the terms *His Honor*, *Her Honor*, or *the Honorable*. Examples of usage are (1) Would you locate the case law in question for His Honor? and (2) I invited the Honorable Jennifer R. Campbell to speak at our graduation ceremony.

The term *honor* is taken from the Latin *honos* and the Old Anglo-French *onur* or *honur*. It was not uncommon for certain dignitaries in the Roman Empire such as Augustus (Gaius Julius Caesar Octavianus) to be referred to as "the honorable one." The British use courtroom terminology such as *Your Honour* as well, so it is likely that we borrowed this term from them as we did parts of their judicial system during the early years of our nation.

6

CUISINE

What Is the Difference between Apple Juice and Apple Cider?

Apple juice and apple cider are both made from apples, but the taste can vary significantly depending on the types of apples used. In general, apple juice is the clear liquid that results from the repeated filtration of crushed apples to remove any pulp or sediment. Apple cider, on the other hand, is darker and more cloudy in appearance as it has received minimal, if any, filtration. There are exceptions to this distinction, however, and the names can be used interchangeably or differently from region to region and country to country. Another term, *hard cider*, is used to indicate fermented cider that is an alcoholic beverage.

Apple juice is typically pasteurized and vacuum sealed for a longer shelf life. Cider is decidedly more perishable and may or may not be pasteurized. According to the Pennsylvania State College of Agricultural Sciences (PSU), unpasteurized apple cider has been a source of past cases of food poisoning, and for that reason the FDA warns that certain populations should avoid consuming cider, populations including the very young, the elderly, and those who have compromised immune systems. Penn State is also quick to add, however, that generations of people have consumed unpasteurized cider without incident! Unpasteurized cider is widely available at roadside stands or farm markets during the autumn.

Apple juice and apple cider are fat- and cholesterol-free, good sources of potassium and iron, and low in sodium. Research suggests that apple juice or cider may strengthen brain function and help protect against cancer and heart disease.

What Are Brussels Sprouts?

The Brussels sprout (*Brassica oleracea gemmifera*) is a cool-weather cruciferous vegetable related to cabbage, cauliflower, broccoli, and kale. Resembling miniature cabbages, this oft-maligned vegetable is actually the leafy, green bud of the plant. The buds grow in a spiral arrangement on the outside of thick stalks at the axil of each leaf. When mature, the stalk of the Brussels sprout plant produces about two pounds of Brussels sprouts.

Brussels sprouts are believed to have first been cultivated in Roman times. They got their current name due to the successful farming of these vegetables in the area that is now Brussels, Belgium. Commercial production of Brussels sprouts in the United States occurs mostly in California, with crops also grown in Washington and New York.

Rich in dietary fiber, vitamin C, folate (vitamin B9), and other essential nutrients, Brussels sprouts are unfortunately often overcooked, which produces an objectionable, sulfur-like smell and bitter taste. If cooked properly, Brussels sprouts are both delicious and nutritious.

Butter or Margarine: Which Is Healthier?

Because it is made with vegetable oils, margarine contains no cholesterol. However, to become margarine, the ingredients must undergo a process called *hydrogenation*. This adds trans fats (unsaturated fats with trans-isomer fatty acids) to the product. Trans fat, largely man-made, increases blood cholesterol, which is generally unhealthy for the heart. The more solid the margarine, the higher the level of trans fats. Therefore, the Mayo Clinic and American Heart Association recommend less-solid tub-style or liquid margarine as part of a more "heart-smart" diet.

Butter, on the other hand, will win most taste tests but contains dietary cholesterol and saturated fat—both blood-cholesterol raising. The Cleveland Clinic suggests that healthy people limit their daily cholesterol intake to 200 milligrams; butter has 33 milligrams per tablespoon. In addition, saturated fats tend to increase "bad" cholesterol, which is also associated with the risk of heart disease.

Because butter was once expensive and difficult to transport, Emperor Louis Napoleon III wanted to find a butter substitute to feed his army, navy, and the poor of the land. Margarine was created in 1870 by Frenchman Hyppolyte Mège-Mouriés in response to a hefty cash incentive offered by Napoleon to anyone finding or creating such a butter substitute. Made of margaric acid (hence the name *margarine*) and other ingredients, margarine has undergone decades of improvement in texture, coloring, and taste. Today, the average American consumes 8.3 pounds of margarine per year as opposed to 4.2 pounds of butter.

How Did Cole Slaw Get Its Name?

Simply put, the term *cole slaw* (or *coleslaw*) comes from the Dutch word *koolsla*, *kool* meaning "cabbage" and *sla* meaning "salad." *Kool* derives from the Latin *caulis* (cabbage). It is believed that cole slaw was first consumed in the days of ancient Rome and consisted of shredded cabbage, eggs, vinegar, and assorted spices. For centuries, cole slaw has been popular in England, Germany, and other European countries, although typically served as a cooked dish. The familiar recipes popular today did not come into being until the eighteenth century as this is when mayonnaise was created.

Cabbage was first introduced to Canada in the mid-1500s by Jacques Cartier. Later, it was planted in the American colonies. By the 1700s, both colonists and Native Americans alike were cultivating cabbage. Cabbage is a nutritious vegetable rich in vitamin C, vitamin K, antioxidants, and dietary fiber and may be served in many ways—cooked or raw. Cabbage has a long and interesting history. Several points of interest are:

- William Collingwood of County Durham, England, is credited with growing the world's largest cabbage. His 1865 beauty weighed in at an astonishing 123 pounds.
- Baseball great Babe Ruth was known to wear a cabbage leaf under his cap during games to keep him cool.
- A French term of endearment is *mon petit chou* or *ma petite chou* (my little cabbage).

How Did the Continental Breakfast Get Its Name?

Breakfast literally means to "break one's fast" from the hours spent sleeping. Different countries have a variety of traditions when it comes to breakfast. Countries in continental Europe typically serve a cold breakfast based on lighter Mediterranean fare and consisting of cereal, cheese, and baked goods—or often simply coffee and a pastry. Therefore, the "continental" in *continental breakfast* is taken from *continental Europe*. Europeans often eat a late dinner, so the purpose of this light morning meal is simply to tide them over until lunch. In contrast, an English breakfast (often called a *full English breakfast*) is a hot, cooked meal that features eggs, a breakfast meat, and tomato or some other accompaniment.

Continental breakfast was coined by the British to contrast their preferred breakfast style to that on the continent. Americans used the term at least as early as the beginning of the twentieth century. Today, *continental breakfast* is used worldwide, especially in major hotel chains, to indicate a light breakfast.

How Did Cracker Jack Get Its Name?

According to www.crackerjack.com, the company F. W. Ruekheim and Brother offered a peanut, popcorn, and molasses treat at the World's Columbian Exposition, Chicago's first World's Fair held in 1883. It is believed that this confection was reformulated soon thereafter to lessen the clumping caused by the sticky molasses. A salesperson who sampled this treat is said to have exclaimed,

"That's Crackerjack!" and with that said, the Ruekheims quickly trademarked the now famous name. Today, Cracker Jack is a product of Frito-Lay.

Not surprisingly, the term *cracker jack* is synonymous with being of superior quality or ability—or masterful, skilled, and knowledgeable in one's field. A typical example of usage is, "Mrs. Barton is a cracker-jack teacher. The children will deeply miss her when she moves to Tulsa."

What Is Curry Powder?

Curry powder is a pungent and flavorful seasoning. It is made from a blend of pulverized spices, herbs, and seeds—notably turmeric, fennel seed, mace, cardamom, cinnamon, cloves, fenugreek, coriander, and cumin. The spiciness associated with curry powder is the result, in part, of adding ginger, chili, or pepper to the mixture. Because turmeric contains curcumin, a powerful anti-inflammatory substance, medical research suggests that curry may offer preventative or therapeutic benefits for those suffering from such diseases as arthritis, certain cancers, and Alzheimer's disease.

Curry is widely used in Indian cooking. The blend can vary greatly depending on the region or the cook. Because curry powder

tends to lose its zip quickly, culinary experts suggest storing it in an airtight container for no longer than two months.

Curry is an English word with probable roots in the Tamil word *kari* meaning "dipping sauce." It has been generalized in the Western world to be synonymous with Indian cuisine.

How Did Eggs Benedict Get Its Name?

Eggs Benedict is an elegant dish made of toasted English muffins topped with poached eggs and ham (or Canadian bacon) and served with hollandaise sauce. This breakfast or brunch favorite likely originated in the 1860s when Mrs. LeGrand Benedict (some sources say it was Mr. Benedict) complained to the chef at Delmonico's, a famed New York restaurant, that she didn't see anything new or interesting on the menu. Chef Charles Ranhofer (1836–1899) quickly whipped up a new dish to please her, naming it Eggs à la Benedick (F. *Eufa à la Benedick*), as it was not uncommon for him to name dishes after his well-heeled patrons.

Another theory involves the dish being named after a stockbroker, Lemuel Benedict, who requested a dish comprised of essentially the same ingredients at the Waldorf in 1894.

What Does It Mean If an Egg Floats in Water?

The shells of eggs look solid but are actually semi-porous. As an egg ages, it absorbs air from its surroundings. The air pools in an air cell within the egg. The older the egg, the more air it has absorbed and, therefore, the more buoyant it becomes. When placed in a bowl of tap water, fresh eggs will sink to the bottom. According to the USDA, even if an egg floats, it may still be perfectly safe to eat. The true test is to crack it open. An unpleasant odor or unusual appearance is the true indicator of a spoiled egg. Eggs may be safely kept refrigerated for about four to five weeks.

Salmonella poisoning is a food-borne health concern related to eating raw or undercooked eggs and a variety of other foods. The Centers for Disease Control estimates that one egg in ten thousand may be contaminated with salmonella bacteria. To lower the risk of illness, purchase pasteurized eggs (if available) and cook eggs until the yolk and white are firm.

Do French Fries Come from France?

Centuries ago when the potato was first introduced, Europeans feared and rejected it, considering it to be poisonous, unholy, and fit only for consumption by livestock. In time, the image and value of the spud improved, with fried potatoes becoming popular in France. Thomas Jefferson, American statesman and confirmed Francophile, is said to have cultivated potatoes at Monticello. He followed a French recipe and called them "potatoes, fried in the French manner," which meant (and still means) the potatoes were cut in long, slender strips.

French fries (often spelled in the lowercase as *french fries*) as we know them today were likely named by American soldiers sta-

tioned in the southern areas of Belgium during World War I. These men are said to have called a twice-fried potato snack served there *French fried potatoes* based on the language of French-speaking residents of the region. They brought their love of this dish back to America with a shortened name: french fries. Interestingly, the French call this form of fried potato *pommes frites*; the British, *chips*; and the Belgians, *frites*.

French fries are wildly popular in the United States and elsewhere in the world. It is estimated that 25 percent of American-grown potatoes are made into french fries, with the average American eating about thirty pounds of fries every year.

How Did Gatorade Get Its Name?

Back in 1965, University of Florida coaches were concerned that the performance of their football team was suffering due to the punishing Florida heat and sun. Team physicians determined that water and electrolytes were being lost through sweating at a faster rate than they were being replaced. In addition, carbohydrates needed for energy were being expended, but not replaced. They developed a drink nutritionally formulated to contain the needed electrolytes and carbohydrates and dubbed this sports drink *Gatorade* in honor of their team, the Florida Gators. Apparently Gatorade made an impact; the Gators had a winning season in 1965 and 1966, going on to win the Orange Bowl—a first for the Gators at that time.

Word spread and other university football teams began ordering Gatorade for their teams—with NFL teams following closely behind. Other sports began using Gatorade as part of their athletic routine as well. Today, it is hard to imagine many athletic contests, whether professional, amateur, or backyard, without Gatorade being somewhere in the picture, not to mention the now-traditional Gatorade "bath" experienced by winning coaches in certain sports.

The basic formula for Gatorade has remained much the same over the years, with certain flavor and coloring modifications to make it commercially appealing to consumers. Different formulations, in addition, are available to meet specific athletic and nutritional needs.

What Is the Graham in Graham Crackers?

True graham crackers are made principally of graham flour, a type of unsifted and coarsely ground wheat flour. They were the 1829 creation of the Reverend Sylvester Graham, nineteenth-century Presbyterian minister and ardent vegetarian. Made of graham flour mixed with honey or molasses, this flat, crisp cracker was marketed by Graham as a health food contributing to an overall sound diet. Graham claimed the crackers were useful in curing alcoholism, limiting promiscuity, and, in general, encouraging a clean and virtuous life.

Graham flour, not always readily available, must be stored correctly and used quickly as it is prone to turning rancid. Most popular brands of graham crackers today are made with refined white or enriched flour, with only limited amounts of graham flour. However, some health food stores offer what more closely approximates the original graham cracker.

How Did the Hamburger Get Its Name?

Ground beef has a long and illustrious history. Genghis Khan's army ate on the go and often prepared meals that could be eaten with one hand. Raw meat was often stored under the saddle to soften it; soldiers retrieved the patty when it was time to eat. Years later, Kublai Kahn, grandson of Genghis Khan, invaded Russia and introduced these patties, which were called *steak Tartare* (after *Tartars*, the Russian name for the Mongols). Steak Tartare became popular in many of the Baltic states.

In the mid-1800s, a similar dish called *Hamburg steak* was a popular dish on German Hamburg-Amerika boats that brought immigrants to the New World. Made of minced beef extended with bread crumbs, onion, and other available ingredients, it was a cheap and satisfying meal. Many iterations of the dish and claims of origin ensued after this point. However, ground beef on a bun, which debuted at the 1904 World's Fair in St. Louis, Missouri, undoubtedly got the attention of a broader audience and created a sensation. It was called a *hamburger*, and the rest is history.

Over 14 billion hamburgers are consumed in the United States every year. Served with or without a bun, it can be garnished with cheese, vegetables, fruit, salsa, chutney, and a host of other toppings.

How Did the Hot Dog Get Its Name?

Hot dogs, an American favorite, are made of beef or pork seasoned with any number of spices such as coriander, garlic, and ground mustard. Although hot dogs are cured, smoked, and cooked before purchase, most people prefer that their hot dogs be served heated. The taste and texture of hot dogs can vary dramatically from brand to brand.

Sausages resembling contemporary hot dogs have existed for many centuries with much lore and legend attached. Bringing hot-dog history into modern focus, most sources credit the naming of the hot dog to something that occurred during a 1902 New York Giants game. Harry Stevens (1855–1934), a concessionaire, was hawking dachshund sausages, a meat dish popular in Germany and the United States, calling out, "They're red hot! Get your dachs-hund sausages while they're red hot!" As luck would have it, a sports cartoonist for the *New York Evening Journal*, T. A. Dorgan (1877–1929), heard the cries and sketched a sausage with a tail, legs, and a head making it look like a dachshund in a bun.

Unsure how to spell *dachshund*, he wrote *hot dog*, and the name stuck. This story is disputed, however, because the term *hot dog* predates this story. *Dog* was Yale University slang in the late 1800s for a sausage on a bun; vendor carts selling this food item were commonly called *dog wagons*, with a heavy dose of suspicion, al-though unfounded, that the sausage was made of dog meat.

Now called *hot dogs, wieners, frankfurters, red hots*, or *franks*, among other names, about sixty hot dogs are consumed every year by the average American.

What Is Pimento?

A pimento (also spelled *pimiento*, the Spanish word for "pepper") is a sweet, red, heart-shaped pepper somewhat resembling a small bell pepper. It measures about 3–4 inches long and 2–3 inches wide with a flesh that is sweet, succulent, and aromatic. However, some varieties of pimento can be quite hot.

Rich in vitamin C, pimentos can be eaten fresh, roasted, or pickled. Canned and bottled in oil, pimentos are available in halves or strips and are available year-round at most grocery stores. This versatile pepper is used as a primary ingredient in pimento cheese and, when dried, is often used to make the spice paprika. Arguably, however, the most well-known use of pimento is as the familiar red stuffing in green olives.

What Is the Difference between Pork and Ham?

Basically, any meat from a pig is pork. An immature hog (domestic swine) is generally called a *pig*, and most pork is produced from these younger (6–7 months old) animals. Ham is a leg of pork typically cured by salt (brine), a dry cure (rub), or smoking. Although the term *ham* is often used for any cured pork product, it is specifically the leg portion of the pig. To further confuse the matter, according to the USDA, hams may be fresh, cured, or cured and smoked. Ham and other pork products may require a thorough cooking process or may be purchased ready-to-eat.

Regardless of the television commercial touting it as "the other white meat," pork is classified as a red meat. The amount of myoglobin present in the animal's muscles determines the color of the

Buddy Helterbran

meat. Myoglobin is a protein that serves as an intracellular storage site for oxygen in the muscle. Because pork contains more myoglobin than chicken, pork is classified as a red meat.

What Is Saffron?

Saffron (saf-run) is the world's most expensive spice by weight. It is made from the tiny bright-red stigmas (also, stigmata) of the saffron crocus (*Crocus sativus*). In fact, it takes about fourteen thousand of these hand-picked, tiny stigmas to equal one ounce of spice. Stigmas are the female reproductive structures in plants that receive grains of pollen.

Purchased in powder form or threads (as dried and cured stigmas), saffron has a unique taste and aroma and a rich golden color about the color of egg yolks. Fortunately, a little saffron goes a long way. It is used in many dishes, including bouillabaisse, paella, English saffron cakes, and Indian biryani. Saffron is produced primarily in Spain, Greece, Iran, and India.

What Is a Smorgasbord?

Smorgasbord is a word derived from the Swedish *smörgås* meaning "open sandwich" and *bord* for "table." However, a smorgasbord is not a table laden with open-faced sandwiches. Rather, it is a buffet arrangement of a variety of hot and cold dishes such as hors d'oeuvres, meats, pickled or smoked fish, relish, salads, cheeses, eggs, potatoes, and other dishes.

Coming into use in the late-nineteenth century, the word *smorgasbord* has been generalized to mean a variety of anything and is considered now to be a perfectly legitimate English word, albeit of Swedish origin. Examples of usage include (1) I can't wait for the holiday luncheon at the club; it will feature a smorgasbord of all my

favorite foods; and (2) Jeffrey loves vacationing in the Caribbean due to the smorgasbord of water sports available to him.

What Is Sushi?

Sushi (sue-she) is perhaps the most widely known Japanese cuisine. Often referred to as "edible art," sushi is a finger-food made with cold, vinegar-laced, sticky rice that is wrapped or rolled in seaweed (*nori*). It can be made in numerous shapes, forms, and types and is often garnished with bits of raw seafood, vegetables, or other types of food. Sushi can also contain wasabi (horseradish), egg, or cooked fish or shellfish—the variations are almost endless.

Sushi is believed to have originated in China. It began modestly in Japan in the seventh century as a method of pickling fish. In essence, prepared fish was placed between layers of vinegary rice and pressed with rocks. This technique improved over time, and the rice gradually became part of the meal. The addition of seaweed came later as a means of keeping one's fingers away from the sticky rice.

Beautiful and delicious, sushi is also nutritious. Depending on the amount of seafood and seaweed used in its preparation, sushi is typically low in fat and a good source of omega-3 fatty acids, protein, and iodine.

What Is Tapioca?

Tapioca (tap-ee-oh-kuh) is best known as a sweet, thick, milky food that closely resembles rice pudding. It is made from the root of the cassava, a plant native to South America and the West Indies. This root, fibrous and thick (and much like a sweet potato in appearance), can be processed into tapioca flour, which is used to make various bread products, laundry starch, personal-care products, and even paper. When processed for tapioca pudding, the starch resembles small pearls. Tapioca is basically flavorless, and other ingredients are typically added to give tapioca its characteristic taste.

Some types of cassava roots are poisonous. It is believed that the ancient Mayans extracted cyanide from raw, unprocessed cassava roots to enhance their weapons—darts and arrows. These same roots were (and are) used for cooking. Fortunately the heating process destroys the poison, making the roots safe to eat. Tapioca is considered by many to be an old-fashioned treat and is readily available in supermarkets today.

What Is a Tidbit?

A tidbit is a small, pleasing, and choice bit of something. The term typically refers to food (I can't eat a whole piece of cheesecake. Just put a tidbit of it on my plate) but can also refer to information (Jan learned many interesting tidbits about dinosaurs at the museum) or gossip (Jessica told me a juicy tidbit about Edward and Sandy).

The term *tidbit* originated around 1640 and signified a small, tasty morsel of food. It likely comes from the English *tid*, meaning "tender," "fond," or "delectable," added to the word *bit*, meaning "small piece." However, there is some speculation that *tid* actually comes from *tide* in the sense of a "feast day." In addition, some recipes are titled "tidbit" as in *ground beef tidbit, chicken tidbit*, and the like. By the early 1700s, the term *tidbit* had evolved to also signify a small bit of information, then later anything small or insignificant.

What Is the Difference between a Yam and a Sweet Potato?

Sweet potatoes and yams are different vegetables, but in the United States both terms are generally used interchangeably, albeit in error. A true yam, related closely to lilies and grasses, is the tuber of a tropical vine (*Dioscorea batatas*) grown primarily in Africa, Asia, South America, and the Caribbean. It has a bark-like, dark exterior and cream-colored, purple, or red flesh. As a food, true yams are often likened in texture and taste to a regular baking potato. They are available for purchase in America primarily in international and specialty food markets.

Sweet potatoes (*Ipomoea batatas*) are storage roots and are related to the morning glory. According to the USDA website (www .usda.gov), *yam* is often used to distinguish the softer, sweeter, and moister sweet potato varieties (with darker skin and orange flesh) grown in the Deep South and California from the drier varieties (with tan skin and yellow flesh) often cultivated in East Coast areas.

The naming of sweet potatoes as *yams* is attributed to African slaves in the South who called the sweet potato *nyami* because it reminded them of true yams from their homeland.

So when you eat candied yams, you are actually eating candied sweet potatoes. Regardless what they are called, sweet potatoes are a good source of fiber, vitamin A, vitamin C, and potassium.

Why Are Some Cheeses Yellow and Others White?

The color of cheese varies between the many varieties available and can also vary within the same variety. In the 1600s, cream was typically skimmed off the top of milk for butter-making purposes. When cheese was made from the remaining milk, consumers considered it inferior, mostly because of its pale color. Therefore, farmers would add flower petals or carrot juice to give the cheese a richer look.

The primary factors that influence the color of cheese include whether the milk is pasteurized or not, the type of animal (goat, cow, or sheep) producing the milk, the animal's diet, and the use of coloring agents. Today, annatto, a tasteless, odorless pigment produced from achiote seeds, is used during the cheese manufacturing process if a more golden or orange-yellow color is desired.

Color tends to be characteristic of the type of cheese. In days past, colorants were often used to disguise poor quality or to mask non-uniform coloration in cheese. However, the use of coloring agents today is usually simply to conform to consumers' color preferences.

7

GEOGRAPHY AND COMMUNITY

What Lands Constitute the Americas?

*T*he Americas are all of the countries of the Western Hemisphere. Often referred to as the *New World*, this includes the land masses and islands of North America, Central America, and South America. It is also used to refer to the islands of the Caribbean and certain other independent island nations. In all, the Americas include thirty-six countries. Of these, the United States has the largest population, with more than 309 million people. Many peoples of the world call this entire land mass *America*, which may cause confusion because the United States of America is often called *America* as a singular entity. Americans often think of the United States as being the only America, but this is incorrect.

America was first used to name the New World continents in 1507, first appearing on a globe and map of German cartographer Martin Waldseemüller. Derived from the name of famed explorer Amerigo Vespucci, *Amerigo* was Latinized to *Americus*. The feminine form of *Americus* is *America*.

What Is the Origin of the Term *Benchmark*?

A benchmark is a standard by or with which something is measured, judged, or compared. First used in the early 1840s, the term comes from the practice of surveyors chiseling a horizontal mark into a stone, wall, or other stationary structure in order to establish a set or known reference point. This cut in the stone was used to hold a metal bracket or angle iron (called a *bench*) on which the surveyor would mount or rest surveying equipment. This benchmark was the place surveyors used for all successive topographical measurements in that area.

Due to its original definition as a reference point, the term *benchmark* came to mean a measure or standard of quality in other areas of life. Examples of contemporary usage include (1) A recent press release announced that seven out of ten schools in Virginia met or exceeded federal benchmarks established by the No Child Left Behind Act; and (2) Joyce used her favorite hair care product line as a benchmark to evaluate all shampoos she tried.

What Is Cannery Row?

Best known through John Steinbeck's novel *Cannery Row* (1945), this road actually does exist in Monterey, CA. However, it was not named *Cannery Row* until 1958 after the novel, depicting the area as a fictionalized setting, was published. Originally called *Ocean View Drive*, this dirt road ran parallel to the Monterey shoreline and connected Monterey to Point Ohlones (called *China Point*). In the mid-1800s, this area was populated primarily by Chinese immigrants who fished for a living. Salmon and Monterey sardines were harvested in great numbers off the coast, which created the need to build canneries to preserve the catch.

The smell associated with the first processing plants, which was bad for tourism, dictated that the canneries be located far from the more fashionable areas on the coastal road. Fish were plentiful and business boomed through World War II but rapidly declined shortly thereafter. By the 1950s, the fish had disappeared—overfishing the likely cause. The canneries closed and fell into disrepair and ruin.

Despite the area's crumbling condition, the curious continued to visit Cannery Row due in large part to the mystique created by Steinbeck. Over time the area experienced a remarkable revival. Trading on its literary and historical roots, Cannery Row is now a major tourist destination in Monterey and home to trendy restaurants, shops, hotels, and historical attractions.

What Is the Chicxulub Crater?

The Chicxulub (chick-soo-lube) crater is the site of a large asteroid strike some 65 million years ago. The impact crater is about 112 miles wide and three thousand feet deep. Located on Mexico's Yucatan Peninsula, the crater remained undiscovered until the late 1970s because it was largely underwater and covered by a layer of sediment. *Chicxulub* is roughly translated from the Mayan language as "tail of the devil." The impact of a projectile of this size would likely have caused mega-tsunamis and clouds of super-heated dust, ash, and steam plus the creation of a layer of particulate matter that, depending on the amount, could have affected the process of photosynthesis in plants and the breathing capability of animals. In addition, shockwaves would have triggered calamitous earthquakes and volcanic eruptions.

Scientists have long theorized that the impact of an object from space caused or played a role in the demise of the dinosaurs and life as it was known on earth millions of years ago. Initially, the Chicxulub crater was considered the so-called smoking gun to support this theory due to its age, size, and geological characteristics. However, more-recent scientific drillings at the site suggest that the Chicxulub event occurred millennia too early to have been involved with the disappearance of the dinosaurs—so the debate rages on!

What Is Meant by *Being in the Doldrums*?

Being in the doldrums is an idiom meaning "to be in low spirits," "to feel sad," or "to feel dull, drowsy, or listless." The word *doldrums* came into the language in the early 1800s and is likely related to the Old English *dol* meaning "foolish"; it was used to describe someone deemed dull or sluggish. Shortly thereafter, *doldrums* appeared in print as a maritime term describing conditions that becalmed sailing vessels; by 1855, the term referred to a specific physical location.

The *doldrums* (sometimes spelled *Doldrums*) is a geographical region also known as the equatorial doldrums, the equatorial belt of calms, or the Intertropical Convergence Zone (ITCZ). Located between 5° north and 5° south of the equator, this area is characterized by light, shifting or rising winds or an absence of wind (calms).

Essentially, this region is bound by two bands of trade winds that cancel each other out. This environment makes sailing difficult, if not impossible, with sailing ships becoming trapped in the area for days or even weeks until more favorable winds prevail. However, this area is also known for its violent squalls and torrential rains, and it is the spawning ground for most hurricanes.

Examples of contemporary usage of *being in the doldrums* include (1) The employment rate has been in the doldrums for years and has stifled economic progress; (2) Erika hoped spring would relieve her winter doldrums; and (3) Ellen tired of Ted's company as he always seemed to be in the doldrums.

Why Do Americans Drive on the Right Side of the Road and the British on the Left?

Back in medieval times, it was common to ride or walk on the left side of the road. Remember that these were often violent and lawless times and roads could be quite narrow, in disrepair, and subject to weather conditions. With most people then, as now, being right-handed, men generally preferred to have their sword as handy as possible, which meant using the right hand to draw the weapon cross-body from its scabbard (a cover sheathe for the sword) on the left. This way the sword would be closer to a threatening person on the right. Wearing their scabbard on the left also kept it away from other travelers and avoided its hitting or getting caught up with the gear of others. To lend further consistency to travel procedures, Pope Benefice (ca. 1300) via edict told his followers to keep to the left side of the road as there were often two hundred thousand or more of the faithful in Vatican City at any given point in time. Centuries later, with foot traffic on the rise in the United Kingdom, the British government passed the General Highways Act of 1773, which included a "keep left" provision that became law in 1835 in the Highways Bill.

Interestingly, there is little evidence of traveling on the left in colonial America, and the reason why Americans travel on the right is unclear. However, it is speculated that the French began traveling on the right in defiance of the Pope; and in keeping with American admiration for the French and the French Revolution—coupled with the anti-British sentiment of the day—Americans began traveling on the right.

What Are the Emblems on the Pennsylvania Flag?

The official flag of the Commonwealth of Pennsylvania is both beautiful and rich in symbolism. The Pennsylvania General Assembly authorized the flag as it is known today on June 13, 1907. This standardized the flag state-wide, especially in regard to the color and positioning of the horses pictured on it, and specified that the flag's background field of blue match the blue of Old Glory, the American flag. This color represents loyalty and justice.

On this blue background, the commonwealth's coat of arms is embroidered. The coat of arms is almost identical in form to that originated in 1778 by Caleb Lownes of Philadelphia. Central to the design is a gold shield (as on the state seal) depicting a ship sailing on blue water, a plough, and three sheaves of wheat. An American bald eagle perched at the top forms the shield's crest, and a crossed cornstalk and olive branch encompass the bottom of the shield. Two black draft horses (harnessed) are located on each side of the shield, and the state motto "Virtue, Liberty, and Independence" is at the base of the shield supported by a gold filigreed scroll.

What Is the Difference between Holland and the Netherlands?

The Kingdom of the Netherlands, *the Netherlands* in short, is a country; Holland is not. Holland comprises two provinces of the twelve provinces that make up the Netherlands: Noord-Holland (North Holland) and Zuid-Holland (South Holland), whose provincial capital cities are Haarlem and The Hague, respectively. To further complicate matters, the national capital of the Netherlands is Amsterdam, which is located in North Holland; The Hague, the seat of government of the Netherlands, is in South Holland.

The government of the Netherlands is a constitutional monarchy and a parliamentary democracy. A rich and varied history and cultural background characterizes the Netherlands. The official language is Dutch, although English is also widely spoken. *Netherlands* itself means "low countries." *Holland*, on the other hand, means "wooded land."

In short, it is incorrect, if not insulting, to use *Holland* and *the Netherlands* interchangeably. It is much like using *Great Britain*

interchangeably with *England*—also incorrect. Imagine using *Tennessee*, or *North Carolina*, or *California* interchangeably with *the United States*—unthinkable!

What Is the Khyber Pass?

The Khyber Pass is a geographical passageway through the Hindu Kush mountain range connecting the frontiers of northern Pakistan and Afghanistan. It serves as a lifeline between Peshawar and Kabul. The Khyber Pass has been an important strategic route for military invasions over the centuries, including those by Darius the Great, Alexander the Great, Genghis Khan, the Huns, the Scythians, the British, and many more in modern times, including those by the Russians, Afghans, Americans, Pakistanis, and various ethnic groups in the region. British Lieutenant-General George Noble Molesworth (1890–1968) once said, "Every stone in the Khyber has been soaked in blood." The pass has also served as a critical trade route over the centuries for traders bringing silks, porcelain, and other prized items from China to the Middle East. Today, it continues to provide a vital passage for refugees and the arms trade.

The Khyber Pass, a narrow, steep-sided track, is thirty-three miles long and ranges from 450 feet in width to a mere 50 feet. Two highways squeak through this tortuous terrain (one for traditional caravans and one for modern motor vehicles) as well as a railroad. The highest elevation of the Khyber Pass is about 3,500 feet. Despite transportation improvements, traveling the Khyber Pass remains a risky proposition.

What Is Machu Picchu?

Machu Picchu, also called the *Lost City of the Incas*, is a historical site located in southern Peru about fifty miles from the Inca capital of Cusco. It is situated about eight thousand feet above sea level in the Andes. Built around 1450 when the Incas were at their peak of power and influence, it was mysteriously abandoned less than one hundred years later. It is speculated that smallpox or a loss of water supply may have decimated the population there, but this is not known for sure. It is considered miraculous that the Spanish conquistadors did not find the settlement, which likely prevented its destruction or sacking.

The purpose of Machu Picchu is also a mystery. Some researchers speculate that it was a colony built to centralize the administrative needs of the Inca Empire or that it served as a ceremonial or spiritual center. Some believe it may simply have been a royal compound for Pachacutec, ruler during the time Machu Picchu was built.

Machu Picchu was discovered on July 24, 1911, by American archeologist Hiram Bingham. Considered one of the New Seven Wonders of the World, it is only accessible by foot via the Inca Trail, by train from Cusco, or by helicopter.

What Is the Mason-Dixon Line?

The Mason-Dixon Line was named for Charles Mason (1728–1786) and Jeremiah Dixon (1733–1777). Both men, an English astronomer and surveyor, respectively, were hired by Frederick Calvert, titleholder to Maryland, and Thomas Penn, son of William Penn, to resolve an eighty-year-old dispute over a hotly contested property boundary between the colonies of Maryland and Pennsylvania. Mason and Dixon traveled to America and conducted their work from 1763 to 1767. At every mile (of 233 miles) along the way they installed twelve-inch-square limestone markers engraved with *M* for Maryland on the southern side and *P* for Pennsylvania on the northern side. Every five miles along the way, larger markers were embedded, weighing between 300 and 600 pounds, that were engraved with the Penn coat of arms on the Pennsylvania side and the Calvert coat of arms on the southern side. These stones were imported from England.

Due to the wear, damage, and vandalism suffered by many of the original stone markers, two surveyors, Todd Babcock and Dilwyn Knott, began in 1990 to locate, restore, or replace the Mason-Dixon Line stones. Babcock is the president of the Mason-Dixon Line Preservation Partnership. According to *National Geographic News*, Babcock and Knott, using a global positioning system (GPS), discovered that the line was off in varying degrees from less than an inch to no more than eight hundred feet, which is remarkably accurate considering that Mason and Dixon used now-antiquated scientific equipment of the day and also the stars to calculate their way through the wilderness to accomplish this task.

The original purpose of the Mason-Dixon Line faded in time. It became a symbolic line that separated free states from slave states in 1804 after New Jersey passed its abolition act; since then, it has been considered the boundary between Northern and Southern states.

What Is Montezuma Castle?

Montezuma Castle is a national monument located in north-central Arizona near Sedona. Dating to the twelfth century, it is an ancient dwelling of the Sinagua, a Native American farming tribe, and is believed to have been abandoned three hundred years after its founding. Although the Sinagua were the castle's last occupants, disagreement exists in the archeological community regarding who built it. Well-preserved and protected from the elements, the castle is a five-story, 45–50 room pueblo ruin carved into white limestone cliffs about seventy feet above ground level.

Montezuma himself, perhaps the most powerful name associated with all things Aztec, ruled from 1502 to 1520, so the castle's name, *Montezuma Castle*, is attributed to early white settlers and now is considered more symbolic of the Aztec people than accurate. Designated as a national monument in 1906, the site of the castle once included a series of ladders that visitors could climb to access the ruins. This practice was discontinued in 1951 due to inevitable damage to the monument and the dangers inherent in the climb.

Why Is *Pittsburgh* Spelled with an *H*?

Pittsburgh has been spelled with an *H* since the city's founding in 1758 and has remained so with the exception of the time period between 1890 and 1911. The name was changed to *Pittsburg* in 1890 by the United States Post Office Department in response to a United States Board of Geographic Names recommendation. President Benjamin Harrison had charged this agency with the task of developing guidelines to revise and standardize naming procedures and conventions for towns and other geographic names. Dropping the *H* from city names ending with *-burgh* or *-bergh* was one of the recommendations.

This understandably caused quite a stir among Pittsburghers, and after twenty years of active disgruntlement, the board relented and restored the *H*. According to the Oxford English Dictionary, *burgh*, *burg*, and *bourgh* are derived from the word *borough*, which Pittsburgh was considered until the Act of March 18, 1816, when it was incorporated as the *City of Pittsburgh*.

In 1921, because *Pittsburgh* was so often misspelled, there was a campaign mounted by Pittsburgh's chamber of commerce calling on all patriotic Pittsburghers to educate the public in the correct spelling of their city's name in order to distinguish it from other cities named *Pittsburg*—cities in California, Kansas, Illinois, New Hampshire, Oklahoma, Texas, Alabama, Colorado, Florida, and Georgia. There is also a Pitsburg, Ohio, and a Pittsboro, North Carolina.

(As a point of interest, there is also a municipality named *Pittsburgh* in North Dakota.)

How Did Rhode Island Get Its Name?

Rhode Island is officially named the *State of Rhode Island and Providence Plantations*. Its name is widely credited to Italian-born explorer Giovanni Verrazano. Sailing under the French flag of King Francis I, Verrazano was seeking a water route from Europe to China. In the spring of 1524, Verrazano saw an island, likened it to the Greek island of Rhodes, and recorded this observation in his journal. This island was later named *Block Island* in 1613 by Dutch explorer Adriaen Block, whose goal was to establish a fur trade with Native Americans.

In 1635, theologian Roger Williams, often at odds with the Puritans due to his advocacy for religious freedom, was deemed to be spreading "Satan's Policy" and was banished from the Massachusetts Bay Colony. Fleeing to the Narragansett Bay area, he founded the town of Providence in an area he called *Providence Plantations*. Others who sought religious freedom and tolerance followed Williams and founded the towns of Portsmouth, Newport, and Warwick in the same area. To protect these settlements from being annexed by other colonies or appropriated by land speculators, Williams traveled to England to secure a parliamentary patent that united the towns into a single colony.

Because Williams and other early settlers mistakenly thought Verrazano was referring to Aquidneck Island as resembling Rhodes (not Block Island), they changed the name of Aquidneck Island to Rhode Island; the resulting charter, granted by King Charles II of England, named the entire area the *Colony of Rhode Island and Providence Plantations*.

Today, *Rhode Island* is used on most official maps, including those of the United States Geological Survey (USGS), for Aquidneck Island as well, but the island is locally called by its original Native American name, *Aquidneck*, to avoid confusion with the entire state of Rhode Island.

What Is the San Andreas Fault?

The San Andreas (an-dray-us) Fault is a geological tectonic boundary between the Pacific tectonic plate and the North American tectonic plate—a boundary that runs about 810 miles through California and into Baja California in Mexico and extends up to ten miles into the earth. These plates move, or drift, at a rate of about two inches per year. Some years, no movement occurs, but when enough pressure builds, movements of two feet or more can take place. The waves of energy that result are called *earthquakes*; these earthquakes occur often and vary in intensity. The San Andreas Fault is composed of a main fault and a number of smaller faults branching from it. Scientists estimate that its plates have moved about 350 miles since the fault formed 15–20 million years ago.

The fault was first identified in 1895 by geology professor Andrew Lawson of the University of California, Berkeley. He named it after the Laguna de San Andreas, a lake along the fault south of San Francisco. He later discovered after the devastating 1906 San Francisco earthquake that the fault ran south into southern California. It was not until the mid-1950s, however, that the United States Geological Survey fully documented the extent of the fault.

It is impossible to predict when the next catastrophic earthquake will occur; large-magnitude quakes tend to occur at 150-year intervals. However, scientists can detect increased seismic activity and can make certain judgments or predictions based on this data.

CREDITS AND RESOURCES

Topic ideas were provided by readers as follows:

Trish Baker: *charley horse*; *sea legs*; *Black Friday*

Ormond "Butch" Bellas: *balling the jack*; *juke*

Jack Berger: cyclones versus hurricanes

Debbie Brehun: blue glaciers; coat of arms; foot-candle

Roger Brown: spiderweb

Don Burkey: spring peepers

Carl L. Campbell: *busboy*

Patti Campbell: birds on electrical wires; falling out of bed; *swan song*; addressing presidents; seeding; when to use *Your Honor*; *tidbit*

Pat Clark Cavanaugh: *lollygag*

Delaney Coleman: loveseat

Helen Craig: *Pittsburgh* with an *H*

Phil Davis: gasoline pricing

Becky Dempsey: snow or ice on car being dangerous; eavesdropping; *little pitchers have big ears*; *pushing the envelope*; *rule of thumb*; apples for the teacher (Becky Dempsey and the children at Valley School of Ligonier); old wives' tales; tailgating; apple cider versus apple juice (Becky Dempsey and Mrs. Copeland's fourth-grade class at Valley School of Ligonier); eggs floating; pork versus ham; *smorgasbord*; emblems on the Pennsylvania flag

Bill Dempsey: Ripley's Believe It or Not; topping out

Ronnie Derk: *bumbershoot*

Joe Domaracki, PhD and Ed Nardi, EdD: yellow versus white cheese

Charles Fagan III: penknife; *stealing someone's thunder*

Kenneth Gfroerer: *sandbagging*

Janet Grace: helium; the *D* in *D-Day*; sporran

Denny Heitzer family: *oodles*; *waiting for the other shoe to drop*; field holler; *benchmark*

George Heideman: *serendipity*

Robert "Buddy" Helterbran: *willy-nilly*; foot-candle

Monica Ivory: English alphabet

Jo-Anne Kerr: straw poll

Arlene Lowry: Tooth Fairy

Jed Lyons: *tally-ho*

Susan McBroom: ants on peony buds

Jack McCracken: shellac

Reilly McKay: french fries

Mike Murphy: birds' feet freezing

Mike O'Neal: lake tides; red eye; *knock on wood*; *marked man*; *windfall*; *John Hancock*; men's pants' fly; sidesaddle

Mary Ann Rafoth, PhD and Carlene Zoni, PhD: *tweak*

Jim Ramsey: *smithereens*

Rachel Roehrig: towhead; *mayday*

Louise Schultz: sun dog

Rick Schwab: *willy-nilly*; blog; curry powder

Michele Schweitz, PhD: *beyond the pale*

Helen Sitler, PhD: muscles hurt after exercise

Joanne Smith: fire rainbow

Ina Mae Smithley: *hooky*

Jessica B. Szymusiak and her ninth-grade English class at Ferndale Junior-Senior High School: Chicxulub Crater

Geraldine Torrence: butter versus margarine

Sue and Bert Toy: Walking up versus walking down stairs

Nathan Turer: *pushing the envelope*

Geraldine Varnell: hyperventilation; *kidnapping*; Khrushchev; lobbyist; presidential duties; presidential executive orders; yams versus sweet potatoes; the Americas

Barb Wallace: CRT monitor

Blanche Clark Weitershausen: ball lightning; blue glaciers; red tide; thunder snow; weather versus climate; *raining cats and dogs*; *rule of thumb*; Google; Harvey Girls; mid-life crisis; P.A. versus attorney; Ponzi scheme; wedding ring on left hand; Cracker Jack; tapioca

John West: pinks

Vernie West: lightning bugs; *sideburns*; *bully pulpit*; *tongue-tied*; Diamond Sutra

Consultants

Mike Briggs, PhD: helium

Steve Kowatch: birds on electrical wires

Erick Lauber, PhD: CRT monitor

Leslie Nemeth: *shylock*

Nancy J. Yost, PhD: blog

Photo Credits

Keith Boyer/Indiana University of Pennsylvania: college/university (Indiana University of Pennsylvania entrance arch)

Buddy Helterbran: pork/ham

Kelli Jo Kerry-Moran, PhD: towhead (of her son, Wayne Moran)

Nadine R. Murphy, Sears Optical: optometrist (of author's husband, Buddy Helterbran)

Dave Rotigel, EdD: *cattycornered*; *swan song*

Richard S. "Chip" Russell: barn (and photo assistance with *mausoleum*)

Helen C. Sitler, PhD: *Cats have 9-lives* (of her Abyssinian, Meg)

Valerie K. Slade: thunder snow

U.S. Library of Congress, LC-DIG-cwpb-05368: burnside

U.S. Library of Congress, LC-USZ62-13026: pince-nez

All other images courtesy of the author.

Models
Marilyn Deller (gray hair)

Ben Helterbran (various depictions)

Research Assistance
Jessica B. Syzmusiak

Website/Organizational/Professional Resources
American Heart Association (AHA)

American Petroleum Institute (API)

American Sidesaddle Association (ASA)

The Associated Press Stylebook, and Briefing on Media Law 2009

The Bible (KJV and NIV)

Centers for Disease Control (CDC)

Drycleaning & Laundry Institute International (DLI)

Food and Drug Administration (FDA)

Google.com

International Olympic Committee (IOC)

James J. Kellaris, PhD

Masters of Foxhounds Association of North America (MFHA)

Merriam-Webster Dictionary Online

National Geographic News

National Oceanic and Atmospheric Administration (NOAA)

National Weather Service (NWS)

Occupational Safety and Health administration (OSHA)
Oxford English Dictionary (OED)
Scientific American
United Nations Security Council
U.S. Department of the Treasury
U.S. Environmental Protection Agency
U.S. Securities and Exchange Commission
U.S. Department of Agriculture (USDA)
Vehicle Code of Pennsylvania

Trademark/Proprietary Acknowledgements
Cracker Barrel®
Cracker Jack®
Dole®
Gatorade™
Honcy Maid®
Looney Tunes™
McCormick®
Parkay® margarine
Ripley's Believe It or Not!®
Shoeless Joe's Sports Café, Fort Myers, Florida
Velcro®

INDEX

ABOUT THE AUTHOR

Valeri R. Helterbran, educator and author, is a professor of education in the Professional Studies in Education Department at Indiana University of Pennsylvania in Indiana, PA. She teaches undergraduate and graduate courses in pedagogy, curriculum and instruction, and leadership studies. Helterbran is a lifelong educator who has taught at the elementary and secondary levels. In addition, she was a middle school and high school principal for almost two decades. She holds a doctorate in educational leadership from Duquesne University, a master of education and an educational specialist degree from the College of William & Mary, and a bachelor of arts in biology from Randolph-Macon College. She was named 2005 Pennsylvania Teacher Educator of the Year by the Pennsylvania Association of College and Teacher Educators.

Helterbran often gives presentations, seminars, and workshops on such topics as Socratic seminaring, professionalism, character education, lifelong learning, and professional development for educators. She writes scholarly and practitioner articles on these and other educative topics and has also authored three books for educators.

Despite these many professional activities, she considers her legacy to be her two sons, Rob and Ben. Originally from Kilmarnock, VA, she now lives in Ligonier, PA, with her husband, Buddy, and black pug, Echo—and she travels to Fort Myers, FL, whenever she can!